Mosaics
THE ART OF REUSE

QUARRY

First published in the United States of America by
Quarry Books, a member of
Quayside Publishing Group
100 Cummings Center
Suite 406-L
Beverly, Massachusetts 01915-6101
Telephone: (978) 282-9590
Fax: (978) 283-2742
www.quarrybooks.com

ISBN-13: 978-1-59253-526-2
ISBN-10: 1-59253-526-7

10 9 8 7 6 5 4 3 2 1

Editor: Shoshana Brickman
Book Design: Michal & Dekel
Page Layout: Gala Pre Press Ltd.
Photographs: Moshe Cohen

Printed in Singapore

Mosaics

THE ART OF REUSE

45 Inspired Designs Using Unconventional Materials

BEVERLY MASSACHUSETTS

QUARRY BOOKS

GALIT GLAZER

Contents

Introduction

Walking through flea markets and browsing at garage sales, my eye is often caught by objects that have long ceased functioning as they were meant. An old wooden clock that hasn't chimed for decades; a pile of glossy magazines featuring items that are no longer for sale; broken china; chipped figurines; brightly colored beads, and more. When I see these items, my imagination ignites, and I start imagining ways of revitalizing them, making them come alive in a new format, and in a distinctive style.

My mosaic works are inspired by a deep sense of environmental awareness, and a love of creativity. I would rather reuse something than throw it out away, and I truly believe that there is a special beauty in things that are old or used. Why throw away a desk simply because it is no longer fashionable when it can be dressed up with funky designs? Why throw away wooden boards when they can serve as the base for fantastic mosaic wall hangings?

As for creativity, I love discovering beauty in unexpected places, and working out innovative ways of expressing it. So while kitchen tiles from the 1970s may not be the height of home fashion these days, there's no reason why they can't be excellent decoration for an outdoor plant pot. As for outdoor plant pots, even when these aren't suitable for holding plants anymore, there's no reason why they can't be assembled into a striking totem pole.

In addition to using and reusing old items, I also love to create unconventional items using skills I have developed over years of working with clay, papier mâché, and more. If I can't find what I want at a garage sale or flea market, I'll make it myself, using pieces of wood, wire mesh, or cement. In addition to building unique mosaic bases using old mannequins and pieces of styrofoam, I also love decorating mosaics with handmade objects such as ceramic tiles and figurines.

The projects you'll find in this book feature an immense variety of materials, but all of them have one common element—imagination. I hope this book inspires you to use your imagination, and opens your eyes to the potential that lies in every old chair, old magazine, or broken porcelain figurine. I hope it inspires you to seek out unconventional materials for making unique and bold works of art that are environmentally conscious, and interesting.

Galit Glazer

Materials and Tools

Unconventional Bases

I hate to see good things being discarded. Why throw away an old lampshade just because styles have changed? And there is no reason to toss away a good wooden chair, just because some of its legs are unstable.

Everywhere I go, I see potential bases for mosaics. As long as the item is made from a relatively durable material, it has the potential to be a mosaic base. Even items that aren't stable to start with can be strengthened using wire mesh, concrete, and a few well-placed screws. Reusing items in my works helps reduce the amount of waste in the world, and adds beauty and interest to the creative work.

Many of the materials that serve as the bases for my mosaic designs are found in a typical home. These items include old chairs, tables, and lamp bases, cracked ceramic jars and flower pots. I also find many great items in industrial areas; these include pieces of metal, discarded mannequins, and more. Browsing through flea markets, garage sales, and auctions is another excellent way of finding objects that can be rejuvenated through mosaics.

Iron enhancements Iron is an excellent material for adding to mosaics. Sturdy and tough, it can be used to enhance a chair back, stabilize a tower of pots, or support a lampshade. Store old pieces of iron in a safe place, and when you come up with an idea for your next mosaic project, bring it to a welder to shape and affix.

Mannequins When a mannequin has outlived its usefulness in a shop window, its life as a mosaic base begins. Cover the mannequin first with cement to make it stable and to provide a surface for affixing the tesserae. You can be sure that whatever tesserae you choose to clothe the figure, the outfit will fit like a glove.

Old furniture Even the most beat-up pieces of furniture can become works of art once they are covered in tesserae. The pieces used in these projects range from end tables with rickety legs to spice racks and old shelving units to which I added legs. With an assortment of tesserae and plenty of imagination, these items can be transformed into fantastic and functional pieces of art.

Planters and pots Just because an old ceramic pot has too many cracks to house a plant doesn't mean it has outlived its usefulness. Covered with a layer of colorful tesserae, ceramic pots can be repaired with style. A stack of several old pots can be turned into a contemporary totem pole. Pots are also excellent bases for small or large statues.

Wooden boards Many people throw away boards when they dismantle cabinets, dressers, or cupboards. Store these boards under a bed or behind a dresser; when you want to make a mosaic mirror or large wall hanging, just cut them to size.

Unconventional Tesserae

In ancient times, pebbles, shells, and other found objects were used as tesserae. Over time, pieces of glass and ceramic objects were used. Traditional mosaics often use glass tesserae known as smalti, or small ceramic tiles that are specially made for mosaic art.

I prefer using found and handmade objects in my work, and my designs incorporate a limitless variety of tesserae—virtually anything that can be affixed solidly with adhesive is fair game. I find tesserae in basements, attics, garage sales, and flea markets. These objects have outlived their original purpose, and are born again in my works. These items include buttons, beads, and porcelain figurines; pieces of mirror, glass, and broken tiles; shells, pebbles, etc. Other tesserae I make myself, using a variety of used and new materials. These tesserae include glass rounds backed with photographs or other images, and a wide range of handmade ceramic tesserae that I make from soft clay, rolling, imprinting, and glazing it myself.

On pages 10 and 11, you'll find descriptions of found items that were used as tesserae in the projects in this book. For a description of the handmade tesserae that were used, please see page 15.

Assorted figurines

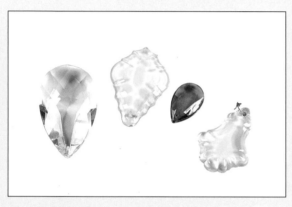

Chandelier crystals

Discarded ceramic tiles

Assorted figurines A favorite china doll with a chipped hand or foot. A collection of porcelain cats you inherited from your great aunt. Golden statuettes, porcelain birds, broken tree ornaments, and more. All of these objects can be used as tesserae in contemporary mosaics. Of course, the objects need not be broken at all, but if they have no more use in their present situation, making them into tesserae is a great method of revitalization.

Beads and pearls You'll never discard another broken necklace once you discover that beads of any shape or color can serve as tiny tesserae on your mosaic work. Pearls are lovely for adding an elegant touch; brightly colored glass beads are excellent for adding tiny bursts of color.

Chandelier crystals are sparkly, reflective, and beautiful. Many weighty chandeliers can be found at flea markets, and though the chandelier itself may be out of style, the crystals are excellent for adding a sparkling dimension to your work.

Chipped plates Is there any household that doesn't have a couple of chipped plates stored in the back of a kitchen cupboard? These are great for using as mosaic tesserae; you can reassemble the broken plates just as they appear whole, or create a hodgepodge effect by affixing them randomly onto your mosaic.

Discarded or leftover ceramic tiles If you live in an area where people are doing renovations, you're likely to be in close proximity to a treasure trove of old tiles. Visit kitchens and bathrooms before the renovators come in, and try to salvage as many interesting tiles as you can.

Fabric scraps Most people have a bag or two of fabric scraps they don't know quite what to do with. Transform these scraps into permanent clothes by dipping them into an adhesive mixture and applying to the mosaic base. You can also use old sheets, or old cotton T-shirts.

Glass Colored or transparent glass is an excellent material for tesserae. Save leftover glass from windows and other objects, or purchase it especially for your mosaic project.

Industrial leftovers One person's junk is another person's treasure. This old adage takes on new meaning in today's industrial world. Discarded items from factories can be an excellent source of mosaic materials. In these projects, assorted pieces of rope are used to make hair, collected metal rings are used to decorate horns, and glass rounds from a shower door factory are used to make transparent round tesserae.

Lace Looking for something to do with those old pieces of lace you inherited from your great aunt? Lace might not fit into your home décor today, but it is excellent for imprinting ceramic tiles, imbuing the tile with a pretty, textured surface.

Mirror This is a favorite material for making tesserae because its reflective natures means that using it allows you to incorporate a bit of the surroundings into the mosaic work.

Newspaper, recycled paper, glossy magazines Papers of all types can be used, either to build up your mosaic basic base with paper mâché, or as a visible

Photographs

surface that can be covered with glass tesserae. If you plan on leaving the papier mâché area exposed, take care when selecting the papers you choose, because it will be visible in the final work. Striking photographs from magazines are perfect backings for transparent tesserae.

Photographs Throwing away old photographs can be difficult, if not downright impossible. Using them to make personalized tesserae is an excellent way of giving the photographs new life, in a unique and visible medium.

Shells, pebbles, and rocks Many people like to collect seashells when they wander on the seashore. These make excellent tesserae (they were used in ancient times as well) and add a beautiful, natural touch to any work. Pebbles and small rocks can also be used to add a natural touch.

Watch faces Just because a watch no longer keeps time doesn't mean it doesn't have something to say about time. These objects make sturdy tesserae that add a sense of temporality to your work.

Other Materials

The items described in this section can be found in most craft shops, and online.

Acetate Use this to cover your background sketch when assembling your mosaic onto nylon mesh.

Acrylic paints These are used to paint the base, and can be mixed with grout to add color.

Adhesives I only use water-based adhesives, since I hate the smell of other materials, and don't like the idea of using poisonous materials to make art. When selecting the adhesive for a specific project, choose it according to the material upon which you will be affixing the tesserae, and not according to the tesserae. Read the label of your adhesive carefully before using.

> **Carpenter's wood glue** Use this to affix tesserae onto wood.

> **Ceramic glue** Use this to affix tesserae onto ceramic.

Concrete-based adhesive Use this to affix mosaics that are made on nylon mesh to their final location, such as an exterior or interior wall.

Household glue Use this to make papier mâché paste for affixing fabrics, or as a simple glaze on modeling clay.

Mixed adhesive made from household glue, wallpaper paste, and carpenter's wood glue This is the material I use for dipping fabric to transform it into a stiff sturdy surface.

Multipurpose glue Use an industrial strength glue to affix tesserae to porcelain.

Papier mâché paste This can be purchased in many art stores, though I make it myself by mixing household glue, wallpaper paste, and water.

Silicone acrylic glue Select a glue that is specifically designed to adhere to metals when affixing tesserae to metal.

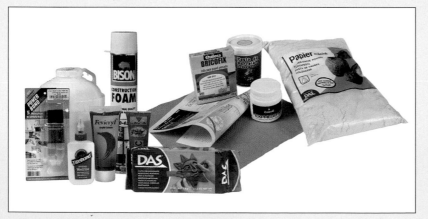

Modeling materials and adhesives

Carbon paper This can be used to transfer designs onto the material you'll be decorating with tesserae.

Cement Spread this on wire mesh to create a surface for affixing your mosaic design. This can also be used to bind objects together, such as several clay pots arranged in a stack.

Glass gems These round marble-like glass objects are flat on one side, making them ideal for affixing to a mosaic base.

Glaze Use acrylic glazes to color clay tiles before firing.

Grout Use this to fill in the spaces between tesserae to create a more even mosaic surface. Grout usually comes in gray or off-white, but colored grout can also be purchased, or made by mixing acrylic paint with grout.

Masking tape This is used to hold tiles together after they have been cut into tesserae, so that the tiles can be reconstructed on the mosaic base.

Modeling clay This is used to build up lips, faces, and other features onto the mosaic base.

Nylon mesh This is used as a base for mosaics that are destined for walls, panels, or floors. Place a large piece of acetate on your work surface, then lay the nylon mesh over top. Affix your tesserae to the mesh, then transfer the mosaic and the mesh to the desired surface and affix with cement.

Polyurethane foam This is used to build up volume in unpredictable and unique ways. It is great for making curly hair.

Sandpaper Use this to make wooden surfaces smooth before affixing the tesserae.

Sketching materials Some people prefer arranging mosaic design as they work; others like to plan everything in advance. If you fall into the latter category, or if you are working on a particularly large or symmetrical mosaic, you'll want to have paper and writing materials on hand, to draw the design.

Spray paint Use this to cover large surfaces such as chair backs and lampshades.

Steel picture hangers Use these to hang your mosaic works on the wall. Be sure to use high-quality hangers that can support the weight of your work, and affix securely.

Steel wire Use this to hold wire mesh in place when sculpting the mosaic base.

Polystyrene foam (styrofoam) balls, eggs, rings These lightweight items can be used to build up the base upon which the tesserae are affixed.

Wire mesh This is an excellent material to use to build a unique mosaic base. Shape the mesh as desired, secure with pieces of wire, and cover with cement to create a stable structure upon which you can affix tesserae.

Tools

The items below are used in the projects in this book. In some projects, only a handful of tools are used, demonstrating one of the many benefits of mosaic art—you often need relatively few tools to get started. All of the tools described below can be found in craft shops or online.

Drill and drill bits Use theses to make holes in ceramics, steel, wood, or other materials. Be sure to select the appropriate drill bit for your project.

Glass cutter This is used to cut glass into tesserae. For really precise cuts, use a pistol grip cutter.

Gloves Wear these to protect your hands when mixing and applying grout.

Hammer and nails These are used to secure materials that are part of the mosaic base.

Paintbrush Use this to apply carpenter's wood glue, household glue, or acrylic paints and glazes.

Marking ruler Use this to draw lines at regular intervals.

Measuring tape Use this to measure dimensions when you are making a mosaic to fit into a certain area.

Micro spatula This is used to apply glue to very small areas, such as the backs of tesserae. You can also use disposable knives or wooden craft sticks.

Safety goggles Wear these when cutting glass or ceramic tiles to protect your eyes.

Scissors or sharp knife Use this to cut wire mesh, paper, and other materials.

Screwdriver and screws These are used to securely affix iron accents or other materials securely.

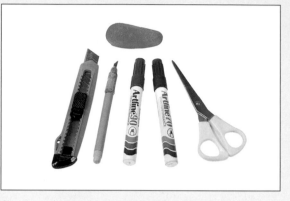

Clockwise: soft rubber finishing tool, sturdy scissors, permanent markers, sharp knives

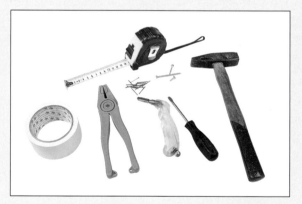

Clockwise: Measuring tape, screws, nails, hammer, screwdriver, pistol grip glass cutter, breaking pliers, masking tape

Gloves

Soft rubber finishing tool This is used to press air bubbles out from under decals that have been applied to ceramic tiles.

Tile nipper This tool is used to cut ceramic tiles into tesserae.

Wire cutters These are used to cut wire mesh.

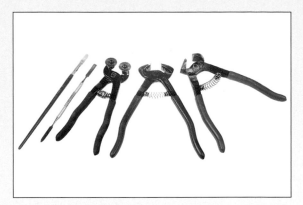

Clockwise from right: Tile nippers, glass cutter, micro spatula, paintbrush

Handmade Additions

In addition to integrating recycled and reusable items into every mosaic project I undertake, I also incorporate a variety of handmade items, many of which are based on recycled materials. These items make the final work even more personal, even more of an expression of my own creative thoughts and efforts. Below is a description of several techniques used to make the handmade additions you'll see in this book.

Ceramic tiles with decals (A) Enhance standard tiles by affixing ceramic decals and firing them in a kiln. To add an elegant look, choose decals with roses, angels, and other Victorian images. To incorporate a playful theme, try using cartoon decals. Ceramic tiles with decals can also be purchased readymade at flea markets and online.

Ceramic tiles with custom-made decals (B) If you have a design in mind that you can't find prepared, many companies offer customized decal designs. Simply draw the design you want, then send it to a company that transfers the design to a ceramic decal. This technique also enables you to prepare decals for tiles according to specific shapes and sizes.

Ceramic tiles with decals and glaze (C) These ceramic tiles are made in stages. The tiles are first painted with glaze, then fired in a kiln. The decal is then applied, then the tile is fired again. If desired, another layer of glaze can be applied, and the tile can be fired again.

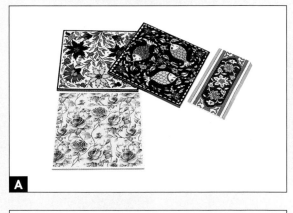

Ceramic tiles with decals

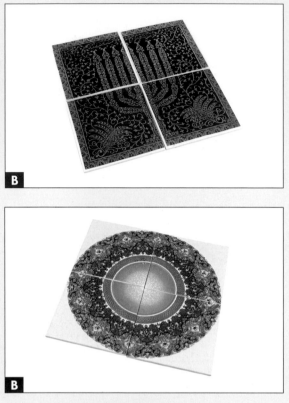

B

B

Ceramic tiles with custom-made decals

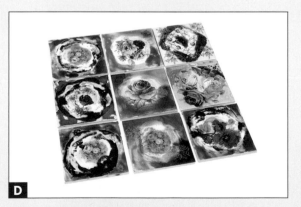

C

Ceramic tiles with glaze and gold

Ceramic tiles with glaze and gold (D) These ceramic tiles are made from soft clay that is first rolled,   then pressed into a mold to form relief. The tiles are then cut and fired in a kiln. The tile is then painted with glaze and fired, then painted with gold and fired again.

Glazed ceramic objects In many projects, I make small tesserae in the form of flowers, leaves, hearts, or lizards. To make these objects, the clay is first shaped and fired. It is then painted with glaze then fired again.

Imprinted ceramic tiles (E) These tiles are made from soft clay, and undergo several stages of preparation. First, the clay is rolled out and imprinted with an object that has an interesting pattern, such as a piece of lace or a metal stamp. The tile is then fired in a kiln. It is then painted with glaze or natural oxides, then fired again.

D

Ceramic tiles with decals and glaze

Round glass tesserae (F) These tesserae are made by affixing images to the backs of round pieces of glass, so that the images are visible through the glass. The glass rounds I use are collected from a factory that makes shower doors. You can search out similar industrial leftovers, or make similar rounds yourself by cutting pieces of glass into rounds. To make personalized tesserae, use old photographs for the tesserae backing. For a less personal touch, use glossy photographs from magazines. To make elegant tesserae, use gold or silver leaf to back the tesserae.

Papier mâché This is a great way of adding volume or height to any work, or to add arms, legs, and other features. Papier mâché additions must dry thoroughly before they are covered with tesserae, so be patient. To incorporate papier mâché, you need strips of newspaper or recycled papier, and paper mâché paste. I generally make the paste by combining household glue, wallpaper paste, and water, but you can also buy ready-made papier mâché paste at many craft stores.

Imprinted ceramic tiles

Round glass tesserae

Basic Techniques

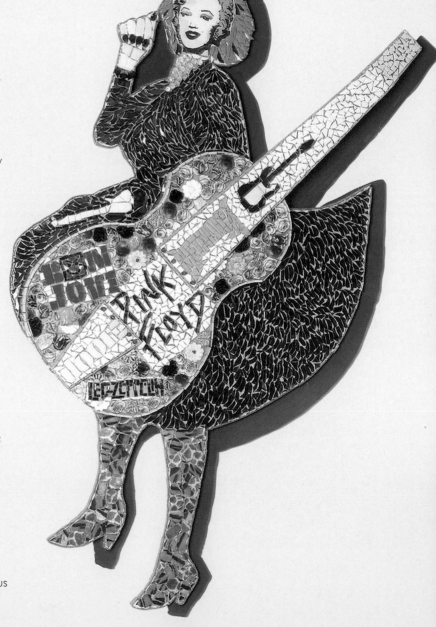

Every mosaic project is unique, particularly when it is made using unconventional materials such as old furniture, mannequins, chipped plates, or industrial leftovers. The steps outlined in the following pages are meant to guide you in your work, and give you a glimpse of how a project looks when it is being assembled.

These steps demonstrate how to make a mosaic sun on a wooden board using leftover ceramic tiles and chipped plates. The sun features regularly spaced rays, and is decorated with a swirling pattern of colors. Red, burgundy, orange, and yellow tesserae are used to make the sun; blue, green, and gray tesserae are used to fill in the background. Although this sun has a spontaneous feel to it at the end, a fair amount of planning is necessary in order to make sure that the colors are harmonious and balanced.

1. Cut a wooden board to the desired size. If you have the right tools, you can do this yourself. Otherwise, have a carpenter cut it for you.

2. Use a marking ruler to draw evenly spaced circles across the entire surface of the wood. Make sure the marking ruler you use has a hole at the base, for holding one end of the ruler in place while the other end rotates to create the circles.

3. Place a sheet of acetate onto the wood and sketch an outline of the desired design onto the acetate. You don't need to copy the circles that are already on the wood onto the acetate, but you can add them if you like, to give you a bit of guidance.

4. When you are satisfied with the outline, begin breaking tiles into tesserae and arranging them on the acetate. You won't be gluing the tiles yet. At this stage, you are just trying to get an idea of how you will arrange the different colors of tesserae.

> This design features two color schemes. One color scheme includes red, burgundy, orange, and yellow tesserae. These tesserae are affixed in a spiral pattern to make the sun. An assortment of green, blue, and gray tesserae is affixed in a spiral pattern to make up the background.

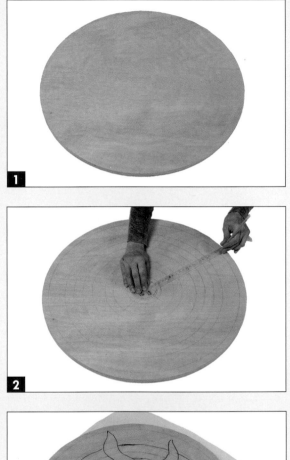

5. When you have come up with a satisfying pattern for the tesserae, you are almost ready to start gluing. First, transfer the design from the acetate onto the wood by placing a piece of carbon paper between the acetate and the wood. Trace the design so that it is transferred to the wood, then highlight the traced design on the wood with a pencil.

6. When you are satisfied with the design, begin affixing the tesserae. In this design, you'll start by affixing the tesserae in the sun first. Start by affixing smaller tesserae at the center, then affix larger tesserae as you work your way outward.

7. Continue affixing tesserae, following the outlines on the wood, so that the pieces fit snugly. Cut the tesserae as you work so that they fit into the designated areas.

8. Affix the burgundy area first, following the swirled lines in the center of the sun, until you reach its rays. When this area is finished, begin affixing the red, orange, and yellow tesserae that make up the other swirled line in this area.

9. When all the tesserae in the center of the sun have been affixed, affix burgundy, red, orange, and yellow tesserae to make the rays of the sun.

10. When all of the tesserae in the sun have been affixed, begin affixing the green, blue, and gray tesserae for the background.

11. Continue affixing tesserae until the entire board is covered.

Gallery of Projects

In the following pages, you'll find a wide variety of projects made from an eclectic combination of recycled and handmade items. Several projects were done by students in my studio, under my guidance and inspiration. Like my own projects, all of these projects are made from both conventional and unconventional items.

Eclectic
Buddha
Clock

16" x 5" (40 x 12 cm)

Position the porcelain birds so that they face inward at the top of the clock.

The golden Buddha figure in this design is both jolly and elegant.

Inspiration

This piece stems from my curiosity about time, and draws upon designs and colors from Eastern cultures. How is it that time has a constant tempo, whereas the tempo of our lives varies? I found the clock that serves as the base for this work in a flea market one day, and the rest of the pieces fell into place naturally. The birds were carefully removed from a porcelain box I found in that same flea market. As for the Buddha, I bought it at a garage sale some time ago, and had been looking for a perfect way of displaying it ever since. In this piece, the Buddha symbolizes peacefulness and tranquility, two themes that are seemingly at odds with the pace and quickness of the clock.

Materials & Tools

wooden wall clock

golden Buddha statuette

golden round symbols

round ceramic tiles with floral decals

chandelier crystals

porcelain birds

glass, various colors

carpenter's wood glue

clock face and pendulum

sandpaper

safety goggles

glass cutter

paintbrush

Instructions

1 | Remove the clock parts from the wooden clock base, and sand down the wood until it is smooth.

2 | Plan your design and cut the tesserae. In this example, the design is symmetrical, so take care to divide the tesserae evenly.

3 | When you are satisfied with the design, affix the tesserae. I suggest starting with the Buddha first, then affixing the birds on either side, with their beaks facing inward.

4 | Affix elements on either side of the clock at the same time, so that the sides are as similar as possible. Insert new clock face and pendulum.

■ Design Tip

This design is symmetrical, so make sure you use similar tesserae on each side of the clock. If you have one-of-a-kind tesserae you'd like to affix, use them to decorate the center.

■ Variations

This work is based on an existing wall clock. To make a mosaic wall clock from scratch, simply cutting a wooden board to size, and drill a hole in the middle for affixing a clock mechanism.

Throne of Memories

24" x 16" x 16"
(60 x 40 x 40 cm)

Integrating watch faces into this design emphasizes its message about time.

Consider the orientation of the round tesserae before affixing.

Inspiration

When I salvaged this chair from an alleyway near my studio, it was a far cry from the magnificent throne you see today. I found it completely dismantled, with all its paint peeling. After assembling the chair, I ordered wrought iron accents, had them affixed, and waited patiently for an idea to arrive. The idea that struck me one morning was to transform the chair into an open photograph album, filled with images of people who are near and dear to me. The photos were taken from old family albums, and selected to represent the transformation of people over time. The theme of this throne is change and the passage of time; this is also represented by the inclusion of watch faces as tesserae.

Materials & Tools

wooden chair

custom-made iron accents

handmade round tesserae,
  various sizes, featuring family
  photographs, images from glossy
  magazines, and gold leaf

watch faces, various sizes

carpenter's wood glue

glass, gold

spray paint, white and gold

sandpaper

safety goggles

saintbrush

glass cutter

Instructions

1 | Sand down the chair until it is smooth. Have a professional welder affix the wrought iron accents onto the back of the chair.

2 | Plan the design of the handmade round tesserae and watch faces. Pay attention to the orientation of the images as you arrange the tesserae.

3 | When you are satisfied with the design, affix the tesserae to the seat of the chair and the chair back.

4 | Cut the glass into rectangular tesserae and affix along the edge of the seat. Cut glass into randomly shaped tesserae and affix at the corners of the chair.

5 | Paint exposed areas of the wood with white and gold spray paint.

Design Tip

There is a round motif in this design that is repeated in the watch faces and the handmade round tesserae. To integrate other round items, consider adding large plastic buttons or round ceramic tesserae.

Variations

This chair takes on a regal appearance thanks to the addition of iron accents. Substitute these with vertical wooden boards, or leave the chair back bare, to create a completely different look.

Garden Lamp Stand

69" x 16" (175 x 40 cm)

Wrap the fabric flowers and leaves along the iron rod and at the base of the light fixture.

Fill in spaces around the flowers and leaves with pearly glass beads.

Inspiration

This striking table lamp features a combination of items that were found and items that were specially made for this project. The base is an old wooden table I found at a garage sale; as for the light fixture, it was incredibly stylish when I bought it in the 1970s, but went out of style a few years later, and has been relegated to a dusty box in my basement ever since. The two pieces are connected with an iron pole I ordered for this piece, and had a welder affix. The pole is wrapped with a trellis of fabric leaves and flowers, giving it an eclectic, natural touch. A diverse range of tesserae is incorporated into the two levels of the table and the legs.

Materials & Tools

round wooden table

custom-made arched iron pole

wide-rimmed light fixture

ceramic tiles with floral decals

carpenter's wood glue

glass beads, blue

wedge-shaped ceramic tiles with custom-made Asian-style decals

glass, brown

grout, light blue

fabric flowers and leaves

sandpaper

safety goggles

tile nipper

paintbrush

glass cutter

gloves

dry cloth

Instructions

1 | Sand down the table until it is smooth. Have a professional welder secure one end of the arched iron pole to the center of the table, and the other end to the light fixture.

2 | Cut the ceramic tiles with floral decals so that the leaves and flowers look like they are cut from paper. Plan the design for the bottom level of the table. When you are satisfied with the design, affix the tesserae. Affix pearly blue beads all around the flowers and leaves.

3 | Affix the ceramic tiles with the Asian-style decals on the top level of the table. Cut the glass into tesserae and affix on the table legs and around the top and bottom levels of the table. Apply grout. Wrap the fabric flowers and leaves around the iron pole.

■ **Design Tip**

Affixing the tesserae on the bottom level of this table is a bit tricky, so decorate this area first. Move on to the top level of the table next, and finish off by decorating the legs and edges.

■ **Variations**

This project is also lovely as a simple end table, just leave out the arched pole and light fixture. For a more elegant look, replace the blue glass beads on the bottom level with pearl beads.

Feline
Frame

32" (80 cm) diameter

Inspiration

This striking frame was inspired by a pair of calico cats that starting hanging around my studio. The base for the frame had been cut long before the cats made their appearance, but I was waiting for an inspiration before decorating it. A carpenter cut the wood for the cats' bodies, and I made their fur using tear-shaped ceramic tesserae arranged to imitate the smooth regularity of real fur. As for base of the frame, it is made from glossy magazine images that are covered with transparent and gold glass. The edge of the frame is covered with mirror tesserae to allow the frame to reflect everyone and everything that surrounds it.

Materials & Tools

- wooden frame (figure 1)
- steel picture hangers
- two wooden cat figures (figure 2)
- nails, regular and gold
- egg-shaped styrofoam pieces
- modeling clay
- carpenter's wood glue
- ceramic tiles, various colors
- glass, yellow and transparent
- glossy magazines
- mirror
- hammer
- safety goggles
- tile nipper
- glass cutter
- paintbrush

Instructions

1 | Affix the picture hangers securely to the back of the frame, and affix the wooden cats to the front. Build up the cats' faces and bodies using styrofoam pieces and modeling clay.

2 | Plan design for the cats' bodies and faces, and cut ceramic tesserae. Hammer gold nails into the faces to make whiskers, then affix the tesserae.

3 | Affix images from glossy magazines to the frame. Cut the glass tesserae and affix on top of the images. Cut the mirror tesserae and affix all around the frame. Have a professional framer mount the frame securely onto a mirror.

(1)

(2)

■ **Design Tip**

Affix tesserae to the cats first. While you're waiting for these pieces to dry, prepare the tesserae for the main frame. Be sure to select tesserae that highlight the colors in the cats.

■ **Variations**

Not everyone is a cat person. Luckily, this lovely frame can be decorated with any animals you like—try adding a pair of seagulls in flight, or two butterflies.

Rock 'n Roll Monroe

47" x 32" (120 x 80 cm)

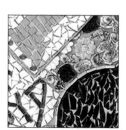

This eclectic guitar combines hard rock music with soft Victorian flowers.

Inspiration

This tribute to Marilyn Monroe is inspired by the famous pose in which she stands over a subway grate in the *Seven Year Itch*. Marilyn's face was copied from a print made by pop artist Andy Warhol. She is wearing knee-high leopard skin boots and a flared black dress. Her right hand shows off a set of shiny red nails, and she is sporting a wild blond hairstyle. The guitar Marilyn seems to be playing is actually a real wooden guitar that I found at a flea market and covered with porcelain flowers, handmade ceramic flowers, and ceramic tiles with flower decals. Ceramic tesserae are arranged in the names of some of my favorite rock bands.

Materials & Tools

- enlarged photograph of Marilyn Monroe
- sketching materials
- wooden board
- steel picture hangers
- wooden guitar
- nails
- hand-painted ceramic tile featuring Marilyn Monroe
- ceramic tiles, various colors
- ceramic tiles with leopard decals
- ceramic tiles with floral decals
- porcelain flowers
- handmade ceramic flowers
- carpenter's wood glue
- hammer
- safety goggles
- tile nipper
- paintbrush

Instructions

1 | Trace the outline of the Marilyn Monroe photograph onto the wooden board (you can increase the dimensions of a regular photograph using a photocopier, or draw the outline freehand), and have a carpenter cut the board. Affix the picture hangers securely onto the back of the board, and affix the guitar, at an angle, onto the front.

2 | Trim the tile featuring Monroe's face, and affix to the wooden board. Plan your design and cut the tesserae. In this example, black tesserae are used for the dress and tesserae made from ceramic tiles with leopard decals are used for the boots. The ceramic tiles with floral decals were cut so that the flowers look like they are cut from paper, and used to decorate the guitar. You'll also need to tesserae of various colors to make the small guitars, spell out the names of the band, and make fingernails and blond hair.

3 | When you are satisfied with the design, affix the tesserae.

Design Tip

The guitar in this design is important, so take your time decorating it. First arrange the tiles that spell the names of the rock bands, then affix flowers to fill in the spaces around the names.

Variations

Though Marilyn Monroe is one of my favorite stars, you might have another iconic figure you want to immortalize in mosaic. Look in art books or online for famous photos of your favorite superstar.

Victorian Vanity Table and Mirror

Table: 38" x 16" x 30"
(97 x 40 x 75 cm)
Mirror: 30" x 35" (75 x 90 cm)

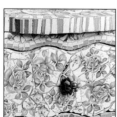

Affix the tesserae with rose decals so that the rose images are maintained in the mosaic.

Inspiration

I saw a book on Provence, France, filled with pictures of elegant Victorian furniture, and decided I wanted to make similar furniture myself, though with a contemporary twist. I bought an old wooden vanity table with an interesting tabletop and a wooden frame to match. I prepared dozens of colorful Victorian tiles using floral decals, and selected green and yellow ceramic tiles to make borders. As for the pretty handle on the drawer, I salvaged it from a bedroom set my aunt had when she was young. These elegant pieces are perfect for decorating any bedroom with elegance and style. Though the decals are Victorian, the style is eminently contemporary, creating an interesting, anachronistic effect.

Materials & Tools

wooden table with a drawer
wooden frame
steel picture hangers
ceramic tiles, green and yellow
ceramic tiles with floral decals
masking tape
grout
carpenter's wood glue
antique drawer handle
mirror
sandpaper
safety goggles
tile nipper
paintbrush
gloves
dry cloth

Instructions

1 | Sand down the table until it is smooth. If there is a drawer handle, remove while you apply the mosaic. Affix the picture hangers securely to the back of the frame.

2 | Plan your design and cut the tesserae. In this example, the ceramic tiles with floral decals are cut into randomly shaped tesserae, and affixed in a manner that preserves the floral images. To do this, tape the tiles together after they have been cut, and until you are ready to affix, so that the flowers are preserved in the mosaic. Cut the green and yellow ceramic tiles into rectangular tesserae.

3 | Affix a border of green and yellow tesserae along the desktop, the desk drawer, and the inner edge of the mirror. Affix green tesserae around the rim of the desktop and the mirror. Affix the tesserae with floral decals on the rest of the surface areas. Apply grout.

4 | Screw the drawer handle onto the drawer. Have a professional framer mount the frame securely onto the mirror.

Design Tip

Tape together the tiles with floral decals after cutting them. This keeps the flowers intact after they have been cut into tesserae, and until you are ready to affix them onto the wood.

Variations

You can use this technique to upgrade any piece of furniture. Use it to transform an unremarkable kitchen table, bedroom dresser, or end table into a unique work of art, worthy of admiration.

A Figure in Flowers

73" x 18" (185 x 45 cm)

Combine a wide variety of tesserae to make a gorgeous garden-like garment.

Make an elaborate ribbon by covering the wire mesh base with gold glass tesserae.

Inspiration

This work is a positive perspective on self-image, and a testament to my conviction that loving your body is what makes it beautiful. To make this design, sketch a figure that is as curvaceous as you like on a wooden board, and have a carpenter cut the board. Decorate the figure with pretty flowers, bright beads, and any other objects that are beautiful to you. Some of the flowers in this design were harvested from antique napkin holders; others were part of a colorful glass light fixture. There are even a few tiny flower beads. The legs are made with ceramic tiles covered with green paisley decals, and colored leaf-shaped tesserae that are arranged like petals.

Materials & Tools

- wooden board
- sketching materials
- steel picture hangers
- nails
- modeling clay
- plastic grapes
- porcelain, glass and ceramic flowers, various colors and sizes
- glazed ceramic hearts and leaves, various colors and sizes
- glass beads, pink
- carpenter's wood glue
- glass, red and gold
- ceramic tiles with paisley decals
- ceramic tiles, various colors
- grout, various colors
- wire mesh
- steel wire
- cement
- hammer
- paintbrush
- safety goggles
- glass cutter
- tile nipper
- gloves
- wire cutters

Instructions

1 Draw the outline of a woman's body and face onto the wooden board and have a carpenter cut the board. Affix the picture hangers securely to the back of the board, and affix the face to the front of the board. Sculpt lips using modeling clay.

2 Plan the mosaic on the upper part of the body first, arranging the grapes, flowers, ceramic objects, and beads onto the chest and torso. Cut the glass and ceramic tiles into tesserae, and plan the rest of the design. In this example, red glass tesserae are used for the lips, and ceramic tiles with paisley decals are used to cover the top of legs. Leaf-shaped ceramic tesserae are arranged like flowers at the bottoms of the legs. Use white and light yellow tesserae to cover the face and chest area.

3 When you are satisfied with the design, affix the tesserae. Apply grout.

4 Use the wire mesh to sculpt a hat with a large ribbon, and use pieces of steel wire to secure its shape. Apply cement to the hat to make a solid surface, then affix gold glass tesserae. Affix a ceramic flower onto the hat, and affix the hat to the head, at an angle.

■ Design Tip

Affix the tesserae that cover the torso and upper legs first. When you're satisfied with the design of your "outfit," decorate the legs and upper body next.

■ Variations

I've chosen a flower motif for this figure, but any thematic collection of tesserae can be used. Tesserae shaped as hearts, animals, angels, or butterflies can all be used to make a unique mosaic outfit.

From Spices to Scents

20" x 16" (51 x 40 cm)

Adding carefully trimmed
rosebuds and leaves makes
this work particularly delicate.

Inspiration

This delicate work is perfect for showing off those tiny perfume bottles that so many people collect, but few people know what to do with. I found the shelves at a garage sale one day—they were probably an old spice rack. I sanded them until they were smooth and beautiful, then decorated them with a variety of tiny elements. First, I cut an assortment of flowers from ceramic tiles, then I affixed these tesserae along the edges and outer shelves of the spice rack. I arranged dozens of perfume bottles on the shelves of the spice rack, transforming the entire unit into a pretty and fragrant piece of art. The pair of ducks at the top stands guard over the contents below.

Materials & Tools

wooden spice rack
ceramic tiles with floral decals
carpenter's wood glue
small porcelain ducks
miniature perfume bottles
sandpaper
safety goggles
tile nipper
paintbrush

Instructions

1 | Sand down the shelves until they are smooth.

2 | Plan your design and cut the tesserae. In this example, the ceramic tiles with floral decals are cut so that the flowers and leaves look like they are cut from paper.

3 | Affix the leaves and flowers on the outside shelves, and on the front area of the spice rack. Affix the ducks on the top level, orienting them so that they face inward. Arrange the perfume bottles on shelves.

■ Design Tip

Place the spice rack in an upright position when affixing the tesserae on the shelves. After these tesserae are secured, lay the spice rack on its back and affix the tesserae along the edges.

■ Variations

What makes this design so delicate is the use of tiny tesserae, small enough to fit on the edges of the spice rack. Other objects that are perfect for covering small areas include shells, pebbles, and buttons.

Antique Automobile Rose Planter

16" x 12" (40 x 30 cm)

Reconstruct the antique cars when affixing the tesserae on the pot.

Arrange petal-shaped tesserae in flower patterns all around the rim.

Inspiration

Plants may come and go, but an interesting plant pot can last a lifetime. If that plant pot happens to feature some antique-style car decals, it may even be a collector's item one day! In this project, dressing up a plain old pot with colorful and creative tesserae transforms it into a conversation piece. Though the design is quite simple, it utilizes several different techniques. The rim features carefully cut tesserae that are assembled into flowers. I chose colors of tiles to highlight the automobile decals on the rest of the pot. The body of the pot features tiles with rose and car decals that are cut in a random fashion and arranged all over the pot.

Materials & Tools

ceramic plant pot

ceramic tiles, blue and green

ceramic tiles with car decals

masking tape

ceramic tiles with rose decals

ceramic glue

grout, green

safety goggles

tile nipper

micro spatula

gloves

dry cloth

Instructions

1 | Plan your design and cut the tesserae. As in this example, cut the blue and green tiles into round and leaf-shaped tesserae. You'll be using these to make the flowers along the rim of the pot.

2 | To prepare tesserae from the ceramic tiles with the car decals, cut out the cars so that they look like they are cut from paper. Then, cut these cars into randomly shaped tesserae, and tape the tesserae together until you are ready to affix, so that the cars are retained in the mosaic. Cut the ceramic tiles with the rose decals so that the roses look like they are cut from paper.

3 | When you are satisfied with the design, affix tesserae along the rim of the pot to form flowers. Affix tesserae on body of pot next, removing the masking tape from the car tesserae as you affix them. Apply grout.

Design Tip

Estimate the number of flowers you'll need for the rim, and cut the tesserae you'll need to make them all at once. This way, you'll be sure that the petals and centers in each flower are similar in size.

Variations

If antique cars aren't your thing, choose tiles with decals in a different design. After selecting these tiles, cut the tesserae for the flowers and petals from tiles that match the decals.

Lounging Lizard

63" x 12" (160 x 30 cm)

Make this pet lizard pretty by affixing tiles with bright flower decals.

Affix the tesserae in rings that accentuate the eyes.

Inspiration

Most lizards dash in and out of my garden before I have a chance to get a really good look at them. This lizard likes to hang around, and never darts away, no matter who comes into the garden to play. Decorated with an immense variety of bright, handmade tesserae, this lounging lizard greets visitors to my studio in a friendly, eclectic manner. The base is built from wire mesh that I sculpted, secured with pieces of wire, and coated with concrete. As for the tesserae, some of them are made from tiles salvaged from old kitchen walls; others are handmade, featuring diverse decals and glazes. There are also several handmade ceramic lizards, making the design even more reptilian.

Materials & Tools

sketching materials
wire mesh
steel wire
cement
ceramic tiles with floral decals
masking tape
handmade glazed ceramic tiles
handmade glazed ceramic lizards
glass, various colors
decorative glass rounds
ceramic glue
grout, various colors
wire cutters
micro spatula
safety goggles
tile nipper
glass cutter
gloves
dry cloth

Instructions

1 | Sketch out a rough design of how you want the lizard to look. You don't need to include specific dimensions, but you will want a general idea of the size of each section. When you are satisfied with the design, cut the wire mesh and sculpt the lizard, using pieces of steel wire to secure the sections together. Don't worry if the connections are not completely secure, since applying cement to the mesh will keep the figure solid.

2 | When you are satisfied with the lizard's shape, apply cement to the entire figure. Let the cement dry for several days before affixing the tesserae.

3 | Plan your design and cut the tesserae. When cutting the ceramic tiles with floral decals, tape the tesserae together until you are ready to affix them, so that the design can be retained in the mosaic. Position the decorative glass rounds at the lizard's eyes, and arrange other tesserae to suggest a mouth.

4 | When you are satisfied with the design, affix the tesserae. Apply grout.

Design Tip

This piece is quite large, and covering it is a major undertaking. Make sure you have several free weekends for decorating this lizard, because it is much more than a one-weekend project.

Variations

Though the lizard I made lives alone in my garden, you can use this technique to make a family of lizards (or any other animals). Try making them in various sizes, and covering each one with its own color scheme.

Beaded
Bride

71" (180 cm) high

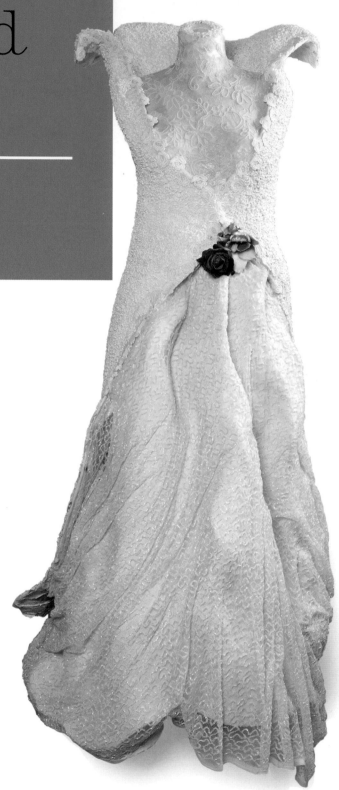

This bridal bouquet never wilts or needs tending.

Delicate lace becomes durable in this sturdy, feminine design.

Inspiration

I decided to make this design after attending a particularly lovely wedding. After all, is there anything more beautiful than a bride on her wedding day? And with this spectacular design, the gown maintains its magnificence long after the wedding day has passed. This dress makes use of an old mannequin, white bed sheets, lace I inherited from a relative, and thousands of white glass seed beads. Don't be fooled by its delicate appearance, though. This dress is solid. The base is made by wrapping wire mesh around the mannequin to form the skirt and high collar. The wire is then covered with papier mâché, white cotton fabric, lace, and beads.

Materials & Tools

- partial female mannequin
- sturdy iron stand
- screws
- wire mesh
- steel wire
- recycled paper, cut into strips
- papier mâché paste
- white cotton fabric, cut into strips
- mixed adhesive
- lace fabric
- Venetian beads, white
- fabric flowers
- screwdriver
- wire cutters
- paintbrush
- scissors

Instructions

1 | Securely screw the mannequin onto the iron stand. Wrap the mannequin and iron stand with wire mesh, using the mesh to shape the gown's collar and skirt. Use pieces of wire to secure the mesh in place.

2 | Dip strips of paper into the papier mâché paste and apply to the mannequin and wire mesh to create a smooth surface upon which to lay the mosaic. When you are pleased with the shape of the gown, set aside to dry thoroughly.

3 | Dip strips of fabric into the mixed adhesive, and apply all around the figure. The fabric will stiffen when the glue is dry, providing a stable surface upon which to apply the mosaic. When the gown is completely covered, set aside to dry.

4 | Plan the design of the lace and beads. To affix the lace, apply mixed adhesive to the desired area of the gown, and flatten the lace pieces onto the area. To affix the beads, apply mixed adhesive to the desired area of the gown, and press a handful of beads onto the area. Affix beads at the top of the neck as well.

■ Design Tip

Take a look at some real bridal gowns for inspiration on how to design your mosaic dress. You may want to sketch out a few designs in advance before sculpting the lace and affixing the beads.

■ Variations

Though brides usually wear white, you can make this dress in any color you like. Try integrating colored lace, colored fabric, or brightly colored beads. You can also add a few pieces of jewelry if you like.

Tribute to Carmen Miranda

71" x 16" (180 x 40 cm)

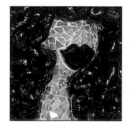

Make big beautiful lips that are as red as you dare.

Create the dress pattern using diverse shapes and colors of tesserae.

Inspiration

In this striking figure, a bowl of plastic fruit is the perfect cap for an eccentric black-haired figure who boasts of big red lips, beaded necklaces, and a suggestively low-cut dress. The figure is built using an old plant pot, a couple of broken teacups, a thick paper cylinder, and the styrofoam packaging that cushioned my neighbor's new big screen TV. I adorned it with chunky jewelry that I found at a garage sale, and am often tempted to change her necklaces, just for the fun of it. This figure is inspired by the famed Hollywood siren Carmen Miranda. Unabashed and bold, it is sure to make people tap their toes and smile.

Materials & Tools

- large ceramic pot
- large sturdy paper cylinder
- styrofoam ball, ring, and assorted pieces
- wooden skewers
- cement
- strips of newspaper
- papier mâché paste
- two teacups
- modeling clay
- polyurethane foam
- acrylic paint, black and red
- ceramic tiles, various colors
- glass, various colors
- mirror
- glass gems
- ceramic glue
- grout, various colors
- assorted necklaces and bracelets
- plastic apples
- fruit basket with plastic fruit
- fabric flowers in a small plant pot
- safety goggles
- tile nipper
- glass cutter
- micro spatula
- gloves
- dry cloth

Instructions

1 | Position the pot upside-down to make a stable base for the figure. Affix the paper cylinder to the middle of the pot to create a base for the body and neck.

2 | Draw the styrofoam ring onto the paper cylinder and position on top of the pot to make the belt. Affix smaller pieces of styrofoam to the ring using pieces of wooden skewer to form a ribbon. Affix the styrofoam ball at the top of the paper tube for the head.

3 | Dip strips of newspaper into the papier mâché paste and use to build up the figure's body, neck, and face. Use papier mâché to construct the arms and hands as well. You'll likely require several layers of paper mâché to make this part of the figure, so be sure to allow enough time for each layer to dry before applying the next layer.

4 | Affix teacups at the chest area to form the bust, and fill with polyurethane foam. Shape lips on the face with modeling clay, and spray polyurethane foam on the head to make hair. Paint the hair black and the lips red.

5 | Plan your design and cut the tesserae. When you are satisfied with the design, affix the tesserae. Apply grout. When mosaic is dry, adorn figure with necklaces and bracelets, and affix the apples to the ears. Position the basket of fruit on the head, and place fabric flowers in the figure's hand.

Design Tip

Make sure the areas constructed with papier mâché are completely dry before affixing tesserae.

Variations

This figure is meant to be fun, so let your imagine play. You can make her a buxom brunette, a fiery redhead, or a blond bombshell.

Weeping Willow Frame

77" x 40" (195 x 102 cm)

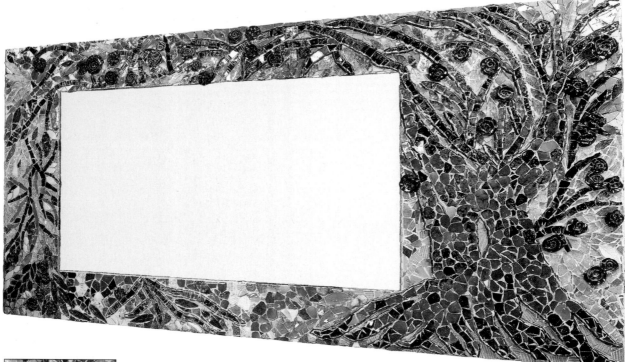

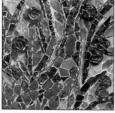

Handmade ceramic flowers
add relief and color to this
impressive design.

Inspiration

This large frame was made to fit around the mirror in the bathroom of my home. The main element in the design is a large weeping willow tree whose branches extend all the way around the frame. A wide variety of tesserae are used, including handmade flowers and leaves, natural pebbles, and several different colors of ceramic tiles. The design represents the transition of seasons. The vivid colors and flowers on the right side of the frame represent spring and summer; the oranges and browns on the left side of the frame suggest the changing leaves of autumn. Pebbles that I collected from a gravel road near my house are situated at the bottom of the frame.

Materials & Tools

large wooden frame

steel picture hangers

sketching materials

modeling clay

ceramic tiles, various colors

glazed ceramic leaves, various colors

glazed ceramic flowers, various colors

glass, various colors

pebbles and rocks

carpenter's wood glue

masking tape

grout, various colors

safety goggles

glass cutter

tile nipper

paintbrush

gloves

dry cloth

Instructions

1 | Affix the picture hangers securely to the back of the frame. Draw a sketch of the tree on the front of the frame, and use modeling clay to build up the bark, leaves, and fruit.

2 | Plan your design and cut the tesserae according to the objects they will represent. For example, rectangular tesserae are used for the branches in this design, and rounded tesserae are used for the tree bark.

3 | When you are satisfied with the design, affix the tesserae. Cover the ceramic flowers with masking tape, then apply grout.

Design Tip

Cover the ceramic flowers with masking tape before applying grout to prevent the grout from getting stuck between the petals.

Variations

This tree is depicted in all four seasons. If you decide to make a tree in a single season, simply decorate the entire background with similar colors.

Golden
Dove
Fountain

24" x 20"
(60 x 51 cm)

Use the top of a decorative teapot to make a truly unusual hat.

Affix the golden birds in a playful perched position.

Inspiration

The large ceramic bowl that serves as the base for this fountain was given to me as a gift, and though it was supposed to hold planted flowers, I had other plans for it right from the start. Its size and wide rim inspired me to make it into a gurgling fountain, and the rest was simply a matter of imagination. The items I used to decorate this work are a collection of odds and ends that were looking for a home. The glass head came from a clearance sale at a store that specializes in unique light bulbs; the hat is an old ceramic candy dish; on top of this is the top of a teapot. As for the pump that makes the fountain work, it was salvaged from an old aquarium in my friend's basement.

Materials & Tools

large ceramic pot

ceramic tiles with floral decals and glaze

masking tape

handmade leaf tiles

handmade flower tiles

ceramic tiles, white

ceramic glue

golden ceramic birds

vacuum from an aquarium

head-shaped light fixture

small ceramic bowl

teapot lid

safety goggles

tile nipper

micro spatula

Instructions

1 | Plan your design and cut the tesserae. To prepare tesserae from the ceramic tiles with floral decals and glaze, tape the tiles together after they have been cut, and until you are ready to affix, so that the flowers are preserved in the mosaic.

2 | When you are satisfied with the design, affix the tesserae around the rim and top area of the pot. Affix the ceramic birds so they are perched on the edge.

3 | Fill the pot with water and place the aquarium vacuum inside. Position the light fixture over the vacuum, place the ceramic bowl, upside-down, on the head, and position the teapot lid on top. Note that because the centerpiece in this fountain is not glued in place, it can be changed as often as you wish.

Design Tip

The centerpiece in this fountain is not glued in place, so it can be changed at whim. Just make sure the pieces you use balance on each other nicely.

Variations

Using golden ceramic birds in this design gives the fountain a regal look. For a more playful effect, use green, orange, or bright blue birds.

Sister with Child

47" (120 cm)

Be sure to affix the bronze snake and rings before building up the face.

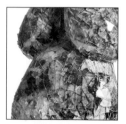

Using transparent tesserae renders the underlying papier mâché completely visible.

Inspiration

I strive to reuse old objects in my projects, and this means that the object itself often serves as the inspiration for the creation. In the Sister projects, I came upon two tall, elegantly shaped vases at an antique sale. I transformed the vases into sisters who are similar, but not identical (see Sister with Coffee Tray on page 54). This sister is pregnant, dressed in a purple skirt, and wearing a bronze snake necklace and several bronze rings around her neck. The rings are similar to those traditionally worn by some Kayan women in Thailand. The hair is constructed by coating ropes with modeling clay, and the figure, made with papier mâché, is covered in a mosaic of transparent glass.

Materials & Tools

large wooden bowl
tall flower vase
carpenter's wood glue
strips of newspaper
papier mâché paste
bronze snake
bronze rings
styrofoam ball
purple fabric dye
mixed adhesive
white cotton fabric
modeling clay
several thick pieces of rope
handmade beads, various colors
household glue
beaded flower
glass, transparent
household glue
safety goggles
paintbrush
glass cutter

Instructions

1 | Position the wooden bowl upside-down to make a stable base for the figure, and affix the vase on top.

2 | Dip strips of newspaper into the papier mâché paste and use them to build up the figure's rounded belly, chest, and neck. You'll likely require several layers of papier mâché, so be sure to allow enough time for each layer to dry before applying the next layer. When the neck is dry, string on the bronze snake and rings.

3 | Affix the styrofoam ball onto the top of the neck, and apply papier mâché to make the transition from the neck to the head.

4 | Mix purple dye into the mixed adhesive until you like the color, then dip the fabric until saturated. Wrap the fabric around the figure's waist like a skirt, and arrange the folds as desired. Set aside to dry completely.

5 | Sculpt a face onto the styrofoam ball using modeling clay. Affix pieces of rope to the top of the head, then coat the ropes with modeling clay. String colorful beads onto some of the ropes, and affix rings of beads to the top of the head like crowns. When the modeling clay is dry, apply a layer of household glue to add a shine. Affix the beaded flower at the top of the head.

6 | Cut the glass and affix on the figure's upper body and neck, covering all of the papier mâché with clear tesserae.

◼ Design Tip

Be sure to place the necklaces on this figure before building up the neck and affixing the head, since they are too narrow to be drawn over the head.

◼ Variations

Dress this figure in any style of clothing you like. Add paper mâché arms (see page 47) or clothe her in a full length tesserae dress (see page 55).

Sister with Coffee Tray

47" (120 cm)

An elongated vase is transformed into a playful girl's dress in this design.

Inspiration

There is a market in the Old City of Jerusalem filled with diverse treasures including bronze coffeepots, Armenian tiles of every shape, religious objects, and more. I never walk away empty-handed from a visit to this market, as the selection of items is tantalizing and diverse. This figure features several finds from a recent expedition to the market. It includes a shimmering dress decorated with Armenian tiles, a headband made from metallic fish beads, and a bronze tray, coffeepot, and cups. The flared dress was constructed with wire mesh and coated with strips of fabric dipped in a mixed adhesive. This piece was made as part of a pair; to see her counterpart, see Sister with Child on page 52.

Materials & Tools

large wooden bowl
tall flower vase
carpenter's wood glue
wire mesh
steel wire
white cotton fabric
mixed adhesive
styrofoam ball
modeling clay
acrylic paint, various colors
household glue
handmade imprinted ceramics tiles
ceramic tiles with decals
ceramic tiles, various colors
household glue
grout, brown
bronze coffee pot, tray, and cups
metallic fish beads
paintbrush
wire cutters
safety goggles
tile nipper
glass cutter
gloves
dry cloth

Instructions

1 | Position the wooden bowl upside-down to make a stable base for the figure, and affix the vase on top.

2 | Wrap the wire mesh around the vase, shape into a flared dress, and secure with pieces of steel wire. Dip strips of fabric into the mixed adhesive and lay on the wire mesh. The fabric will stiffen when the glue is dry, providing a stable surface upon which to apply the mosaic. When the dress is completely covered, set aside to dry.

3 | Affix the styrofoam ball to the top of the vase and sculpt the head, hair, and a flat base for supporting the coffee tray. When the clay is dry, paint facial features. Allow the paint to dry, then apply a layer of household glue to add a shine.

4 | Cut the tesserae and plan the design of the dress. When you are satisfied with the design, affix the tesserae. Apply grout. Hang the fish beads around the top of the head. Affix the coffee cups and pot to the tray, then affix the tray to the top of the head.

Design Tip

Practice sculpting the face in advance, because getting the right dimensions can be challenging. You may even want to sculpt the face onto the styrofoam ball before affixing it to the vase.

Variations

If coffee isn't your thing, replace the coffee pot and cups with a flower vase, potted plant, or straw basket with plastic (or fresh) fruit.

Classic Round Table

28" x 24"
(71 cm diameter x 61 cm height)

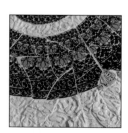

Intersperse carefully cut roses
on the surface of this table.

Inspiration

The base for this elegant piece of furniture is actually a rickety old table I found on the side of the road. It had failed to sell at a garage sale, I think, and was left in the trash by its previous owners. The legs were uneven and the surface was nicked and chipped. Covering the table with handmade lace tesserae and including a floral center transformed it from a garage sale reject to a fine piece of furniture, a work of art worthy of taking center stage in any room. Most of the tesserae in this design were made from handmade tiles that were imprinted with lace and coated with cream-colored glaze. These tiles are stunning to see and remarkable to touch.

Materials & Tools

wooden table

ceramic tiles with rose decals

round ceramic tiles with oriental-style decals

masking tape

handmade imprinted ceramic tiles

carpenter's wood glue

grout, cream-colored

sandpaper

safety goggles

tile nipper

paintbrush

gloves

dry cloth

Instructions

1 | Sand down the table until it is smooth.

2 | Plan your design and cut the tesserae. In this example, the ceramic tiles with rose decals are cut so that the roses look like they are cut from paper. When cutting the round ceramic tiles with Asian-style decals, tape the tiles together after they have been cut into tesserae until you are ready to affix, so that the design can be retained in the mosaic.

3 | When you are satisfied with the design, affix the tesserae. Apply grout.

■ **Design Tip**

Think about the room where this table will be placed, and select tiles with decals that match the décor. Make sure you cover the entire surface of the table, including all sides of the table legs.

■ **Variations**

If you decide to cover a square table with tesserae, choose square ceramic tiles for making the centerpiece. You can also affix tesserae from tiles with decals along the outer edge of the legs.

Leaping Leopard Desk

51" x 32" x 20"
(130 x 81 x 51 cm)

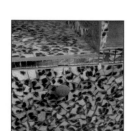

Add sparkle to this striking desk by affixing gold tesserae along the edges.

Inspiration

An unusual wall unit I found on the street inspired this piece. I didn't want to use it as a wall unit, and decided that if I attached a pair of sturdy legs, it could function perfectly as a desk. I ordered a set of legs from the carpenter, and had them attached. I sanded down the entire desk, and dressed it with tesserae. The top of the desk features tesserae from tiles with leopard decals, and the legs are covered with black tesserae. Thick rays of gold glass were arranged on two sides of the desk, evocative of a tiger's stripes. Black tesserae were used to decorate the legs, and gold glass tesserae were affixed along the edges of the desk and one of the drawers.

Materials & Tools

wooden desk (or wooden wall unit and legs, attached)

ceramic tiles with leopard decals

ceramic tiles, black

glass, gold

carpenter's wood glue

grout, brown

sandpaper

safety goggles

tile nipper

glass cutter

paintbrush

gloves

dry cloth

Instructions

1 | Sand down the desk until it is smooth.

2 | Plan your design and cut the tesserae. In this example, tesserae made from ceramic tiles with leopard decals are used to decorate the desk and two of the drawers; tesserae made from black tiles are used to decorate the legs. Triangular pieces of gold glass are used to decorate the sides of the desk, and rectangular gold tesserae are affixed along the edges of the desk and on one of the drawers.

3 | When you are satisfied with the design, affix the tesserae. Apply grout.

Design Tip

Remove the drawer handles before affixing the tesserae so you can access the entire surface of the drawers. Affix the gold tesserae first, then affix the tesserae with the leopard decals all around.

Variations

This desk looks striking in any animal pattern. If you select decals with zebra stripes, use black, white, or silver glass for the edges.

Angels and Dolls Lamp

20" x 10" (51 cm x 25 cm)

A pair of angels is surrounded by pretty roses and bright beads.

Bring a bit of magic to your work by integrated tiny fairies.

Inspiration

One of my daughters is crazy about fairies. She must have well over 100 of them in her collection. Not content to leave the fairies to gather dust on a shelf, my daughter handles them often, and they sometimes get chipped wings and broken hands. Luckily, even chipped fairies don't lose their magic; some of my favorites are assembled right here in this playful lamp. There are also angels, tiny ceramic animal figures, handmade ceramic leaves, butterflies, roses, gold pendants, brightly colored plastic beads, and pearls in a variety of sizes. As for the lampshade, I painted an ordinary white one with gold spray paint.

Materials & Tools

ceramic table lamp
porcelain fairies
handmade ceramic flowers
handmade ceramic leaves
ceramic animal figures
gold pendants, backings removed
multipurpose glue with dispenser
plastic beads, various colors
pearls, various sizes
white lampshade
gold spray paint

Instructions

1 | Plan the design of your tesserae. When you have a general idea of how to arrange the elements, begin affixing the tesserae. Start with the larger tesserae first, and consider their orientation as you affix them, and their immediate surroundings. For example, if you are affixing a pair of porcelain fairies, consider where they are facing, and what objects are around them.

2 | When you have affixed all the large tesserae, fill in the spaces with smaller tesserae, such as the small animal figures, beads, and pearls.

3 | Spray the lampshade with gold paint, then affix at the top of the lamp.

■ Design Tip

Affix the larger tesserae including the fairies, leaves, and figurines first, then fill in the spaces with smaller tesserae.

■ Variations

You can also make a fabulous lamp by covering it with buttons of every size, coins, or shells, or rocks and pebbles. Use mirror tesserae in various sizes for a funky, reflective look.

Rose and Crystal Wall Sconce

16" x 8" (40 x 20 cm)

Inspiration

This elegant wall sconce features an assortment of found objects and handmade items, all of which are mounted on an arched sheet of steel that can be hung in front of a regular wall light. The handmade tiles at the top feature a relief of swirling flowers that is painted with a pearly pink glaze and decorated with gold. Below this is an arrangement of handmade ceramic roses, interspersed with pink glass beads. The bottom of the sconce features chunks of beige glass, and below this is a selection of crystals that were salvaged from an old chandelier. The overall affect is elegant yet eclectic, one that combines the precision of crystals with the unpredictable beauty of handmade roses.

Materials & Tools

arched piece of steel sheet

steel picture hangers

silicone acrylic glue with dispenser

handmade ceramic tiles with glaze and gold

glass, beige

handmade ceramic roses

glass beads, pink

chandelier crystals

steel eye pins

drill and metal drill bit

safety goggles

glass cutter

micro spatula

Instructions

1 | Drill nine evenly spaced holes along the bottom of the steel sheet. Affix the picture hangers to the back of the sheet.

2 | Plan your design and cut the tesserae. In this example, the tiles at the top of the sconce were cut to size before they were fired, so they are a perfect fit. Cut the glass into small rectangular tesserae.

3 | When you are satisfied with the design, affix the tesserae. String the chandelier crystals onto the eye pins and hang from the holes at the bottom of the steel sheet.

■ Design Tip

Affix the tesserae at the top of the sconce first, since they are made to fit the steel sheet. Add the roses, glass beads, and beige glass tesserae to fill the entire surface of the sconce.

■ Variations

If you don't have chandelier crystals to dangle, that's just fine. You can also use large glass or pearl beads, decorative ornaments, or coins with holes drilled at two ends.

Bird
of a
Feather

47" (120 cm), including 32"
(80 cm) legs

Add an unusual necklace
to enhance this bird's
mysterious look.

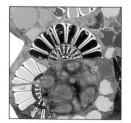

Use tiles with round designs to
accentuate the shape of this
bird's tail feathers.

Inspiration

This exotic bird was born out of a desire to brighten up my garden. It was wintertime, things were bleak, and I felt that a peacock-inspired bird was just what my garden needed. I sculpted the body of the bird from clay, and shaped round feathers on the back and a curved beak. I also included several small holes in the top, for inserting the ceramic "hair." I ordered wrought iron legs that would be skinny but sturdy enough to support the ceramic body and mosaic tesserae. To enhance the bird's already exotic appearance, I added a bronze face that was brought to me as a souvenir from Thailand, and several rings around the neck.

Materials & Tools

bird-shaped ceramic body, with several small holes on the head

custom-made iron legs

multipurpose glue with dispenser

ceramic tiles, various colors

handmade ceramic roses

heart-shaped ceramic tiles

small ceramic birds

ceramic glue

handmade ceramic balls with wires

thick steel wire

large bronze face pendant

grout, blue

safety goggles

tile nipper

micro spatula

gloves

dry cloth

Instructions

1 | Affix the ceramic body onto the iron legs. Cut the tesserae and plan your design.

2 | When you are satisfied with the design, affix the tesserae onto the body and head of the bird. In this example, round tesserae are used to make the eyes, and each eye is surrounded with a ring of handmade ceramic roses. Heart-shaped ceramic tiles are affixed at the base of the head. Ceramic balls with wires are inserted into the holes at the top of the head. Affix the ceramic birds at the top of the head. Apply grout.

3 | To decorate the neck area, twist the wire around the neck several times. String the bronze face onto the wire, position it at the front of the bird, then continue wrapping the wire until you reach the body. Secure the wire by twisting the ends together firmly.

▪ Design Tip

Wind the steel wire around the bird's neck before affixing the tesserae so you'll know where to start affixing the tesserae for the head and the body.

▪ Variations

Replace the handmade ceramic bird with a store-bought figure if you like. Sketch out your design in advance, and cut the tesserae in a manner that complements the bird's shape.

Ringed Leader

63" x 16" (160 x 41 cm)

Small ceramic leaves and flowers are used to decorate the topmost ring.

Select grout that matches the tesserae you select for each ring.

Inspiration

This striking figure is made from a stack of handmade clay rings, each of which has a distinct design and color scheme. Most of the rings feature eyes and a nose, though the third ring from the bottom is decorated with large ceramic leaves, and the top ring features an entire face. The rings are decorated with handmade ceramic flowers and leaves, glass beads, and diverse types of tesserae. The topmost ring is topped by a horned cap with coiled iron wires that was specially made for this piece. The horns are decorated with an assortment of metal rings and several small birds are affixed between the coiled wires, frolicking as though in a birdbath.

Materials & Tools

seven handmade ceramic rings

ceramic tiles, various colors

handmade ceramic flowers

handmade ceramic leaves

handmade imprinted ceramic tiles

glass gems

ceramic glue

custom-made iron headpiece, with
  horns and curled hair

metal rings, various sizes

small ceramic birds

silicone acrylic glue with dispenser

grout, various colors

concrete

safety goggles

tile nipper

micro spatula

gloves

dry cloth

gloves

Instructions

1 | Plan the mosaic design for each ring. Be sure to consider the color of the grout you'll use, and the types of tesserae.

2 | When you are satisfied with the designs, cut the tesserae, and affix. Affix the headpiece onto one of the rings. String metal rings onto the horns, and affix ceramic birds on the top of the headpiece. Apply grout.

3 | Arrange the rings in a stack. When you are satisfied with the arrangement, affix the rings to each other with concrete.

Design Tip

Decorate each of the rings in advance, and give them time to dry before arranging them in a stack. Insert a steel pole in the middle to strengthen the pole, and make sure it doesn't topple.

Variations

This concept can be used to make any type of tall design. Try constructing a multi-tiered tree by creating rings decorated with different fruits and flowers.

Women in the Windows

35" x 28" (89 x 71 cm)

This extraordinary design is based on the door of an ordinary kitchen cabinet.

Inspiration

This work is based on a four-paned cabinet front that I found in the street, likely discarded due to kitchen renovations. The frame is decorated with the figures of two women, in two different poses. The frame features two large ceramic leaves, a smaller frame painted gold, and an assortment of tesserae. The images affixed on the women's faces were taken from glossy magazines. The woman in the top right corner sports a black hairdo, and gazes outwards with confidence. The woman in the bottom corner is wearing a mosaic headpiece and has her eyes cast downward. Each of the windowpanes is backed with a piece of colored glass, as are the faces of the women.

Materials & Tools

wooden kitchen cabinet door, boards, and picture frame

sketching materials

steel picture hangers

nails

glass sheets, various colors

carpenter's wood glue

glossy magazines

ceramic tiles, various colors, with floral decals

gold spray paint

handmade ceramic leaves and bird

grout, various colors

sandpaper

hammer

paintbrush

safety goggles

tile nipper

glass cutter

gloves

dry sponge

Instructions

1 | Sand down the cabinet door until it is smooth. Draw the shapes of two figures onto the wooden boards and have a carpenter cut out the figures. Secure the figures onto the front of the cabinet door. Affix the picture hangers and sheets of colored glass to the back of the cabinet door.

2 | Plan your design and cut the tesserae. In this example, the faces are made from images cut from magazines, then covered with colored glass. Leaf-shaped tesserae are used to make one of the figure's dresses, and triangular tesserae are used to make the other figure's body and bikini top. Cut tesserae for the hair and hair piece, as well.

3 | When you are satisfied with your designs, affix the tesserae. Paint the small wooden picture frame gold and affix in the top left corner. Affix the ceramic bird and leaf.

4 | Cut the ceramic tiles with floral decals so that the flowers and leaves look like they are cut from paper, and affix along the exposed surface of the cabinet. Apply grout.

Design Tip

Consider the shape of the tesserae you use to dress the two wooden figures. When affixing the rose tesserae to the cabinet door, allow them to extend a bit over the edges.

Variations

You can replace the female figures here with any other figures you like. Try cutting the wooden boards in the shapes of children, animals, or images from nature, and affix tesserae to match.

Tzofi Peled

The Mirrors Make the Man

71" (180 cm) high

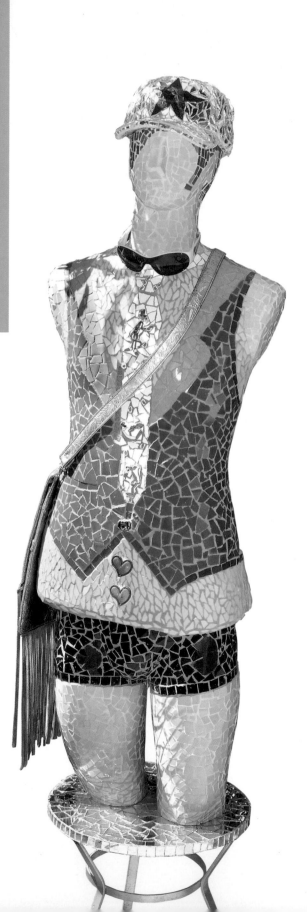

This mannequin includes a
buttoned strap along the back.

Inspiration

This figure is based on a mannequin that used to be in the window of a men's clothing store. The shop owners retired, and the store was taken over by a flower shop that didn't need a male mannequin. The figure was left on the sidewalk one afternoon, and moved into my studio that evening. It is now dressed with an eclectic assortment of clothing, including black shorts with hearts, a white tie with Pink Panther decals, and a mirrored baseball cap. The sunglasses and silvery handbag are a tribute to the mannequin's new life, far removed from his staid past of white dress shirts and ties. The mannequin is affixed to a small round end table covered with mirrored mosaic, a reflection of its bright future.

Materials & Tools

- partial male mannequin
- small round table
- cement
- styrofoam ball
- polyurethane foam
- ceramic tiles, various colors
- ceramic tiles with Pink Panther decals
- heart-shaped silver buttons
- ceramic glue
- mirror
- baseball cap
- grout, various colors
- sunglasses
- silver handbag
- hammer and nails
- micro spatula
- safety goggles
- tile nipper
- glass cutter
- gloves
- dry cloth

Instructions

1 | Securely affix the mannequin onto the table. Affix the styrofoam ball to the top of the neck for the head, and construct a nose using a bit of polyurethane foam.

2 | Plan your design and cut the tesserae. In this example, heart-shaped red tesserae and black tesserae are used for the shorts, yellow tesserae are used to make the shirt, and purple and pink tesserae are used to make the vest. Ceramic tiles with Pink Panther decals are used to make the tie and large silver heart-shaped buttons are affixed on the middle of the shirt. Use flesh colored tesserae to cover the legs, arms, neck and head, and use brown tesserae to make the hair.

3 | Dip the hat into the cement and position on top of the head. When the hat is dry, affix red tesserae in a star shape, and cover the rest of the hat with mirror tesserae. Cover the table with mirror tesserae as well. Apply grout. Add sunglasses and handbag.

■ Design Tip

Draw a sketch of this mannequin's clothing before affixing the tesserae. When adding accessories, you can leave them unadorned (see the purse and sunglasses) or give them a mosaic exterior (see the baseball cap).

■ Variations

Dress your mannequin any way you like. Put on a ceramic bikini for the beach, a glittery gown for an evening out, or a silly costume. Be sure to select fun accessories that match.

Moshit Segal

Totem with Fish

75" x 12" (190 x 30 cm)

Round tesserae are used for the center, and leaflike tesserae are used for the petals.

One pot features glass gems affixed in a wave pattern, and ceramic flowers.

Inspiration

Indigenous peoples in North America have been carving totem poles for generations. Some totem poles tell legendary stories, others convey family lineage; some totem poles mark notable events; others are carved simply for beauty. This mosaic totem is designed to add beauty and brightness to the house it adorns. It features vibrant colors and carefree designs, and includes pieces of mirror to reflect the light of the sun, and the surrounding environment. This design is a great way to transform broken ceramic pots and planters into an impressive and expressive structure. Be sure to support the totem with a sturdy iron rod so that it doesn't tumble.

Materials & Tools

- ceramic pots and planters, various sizes and shapes
- ceramic fish figure
- metal rod with a sturdy base
- cement
- ceramic tiles, various colors
- round ceramic tiles with Armenian-style decals
- ceramic tiles with floral decals
- handmade flower tiles
- handmade leaf tiles
- handmade fish tiles
- glass gems, various sizes and colors
- mirror
- ceramic glue
- grout, various colors
- diamond-tipped drill
- micro spatula
- safety goggles
- tile nipper
- glass cutter
- gloves
- dry cloth

Instructions

1 | Drill holes in some of the pots. These holes are like windows in the pots, and add an extra dimension for your decoration.

2 | Arrange the pots into a pole by stacking one on top of the other, turning some of them upside down and leaving others upright. Be sure to position a large inverted pot on the bottom, for a stable base, and position the fish figure on the top.

3 | When you are satisfied with the arrangement of the pots, string them onto the metal pole and affix with cement.

4 | Plan the design for each pot and cut the tesserae. Each pot is designed separately, and has a complete motif of its own. When you are satisfied with the designs, affix the tesserae. Apply grout.

Design Tip

Ensure every pot has a hole in the bottom and top, for inserting the metal rod. When decorating the pots, keep the bottom and top rims bare so that they can be affixed in a stack.

Variations

In this design, every planter has its own theme. You may also choose to decorate the pots in related themes; for example, decorating each one with a different flower motif, or using tesserae of a single color in each pot.

Yuniah Goldwasser

Wheatfield

51" x 16" x 16"
(130 x 40 x 40 cm)

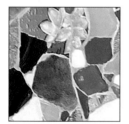

Combine different shades and shapes of blue tesserae to make a vibrant sky.

Green beads are arranged to resemble wheat kernels ready for harvest.

Inspiration

This work commands a presence, both for its size and for the diversity of its tesserae. The sides are covered with large, irregularly shaped tesserae in earthy hues of brown, at the bottom, and airy shades of blue at the top. The tesserae were collected from a variety of sources, including an old kitchen I discovered just days before its demolition. Some of the tesserae are textured, others are smooth; some are glittery and bright, others are earthy and rich. Bright yellows and gold are used to make the wheat sheaves, and green glass beads are used to make the seeds. The tesserae on the top of the column are arranged in the shape of a sun.

Materials & Tools

four-sided wooden column
sketching materials
ceramic tiles, various colors
glass beads, green
carpenter's wood glue
grout, various colors
safety goggles
tile nipper
glass cutter
paintbrush
gloves
dry cloth

Instructions

1 | Draw a sketch of your design onto the wooden column.

2 | Plan the design, and cut the tesserae according to the objects they will represent. In this design, long, thin tesserae are used to make the stalk, and rounded, irregularly shaped tesserae are used for the background. Rectangular tesserae are used at the base of the column, and to make the wheat stems.

3 | When you are satisfied with the design, affix the tesserae. Apply grout.

Design Tip

Affix the beads that make up the wheat kernels first, then affix the long, straight tesserae that extend outward from each sheaf.

Variations

This four-sided column is excellent for displaying a variety of thematic images. Try decorating each side with images from different seasons or different holidays.

Yuniah Goldwasser

Date Palm Wall Hanging

36" x 20" (91 x 51 cm)

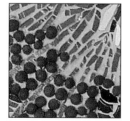

Shape dates using modeling clay and affix in a natural-looking pattern.

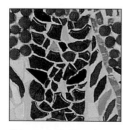

Cut ceramic tiles in various rounded shapes to mimic the texture of date palm tree bark.

Inspiration

This vibrant design features a date palm tree laden with large brown dates that are ripe and ready to eat. All of the tesserae were cut specifically for the elements they represent. For example, the leaves are made from diverse shades of green tiles, cut into leaf-shaped tesserae. The branches supporting the dates are made from rectangular yellow tesserae. The tesserae used to make the tree bark are cut into pebble-like shapes, giving a textured surface similar to a real date palm bark. The background is made from triangular tesserae cut from glossy white ceramic tiles. As for the dates, these are shaped from modeling clay, and flattened on one side, so that they can be firmly affixed to the board.

Materials & Tools

wooden board
steel picture hangers
sketching materials
ceramic tiles, various colors
modeling clay
acrylic paint, brown
carpenter's wood glue
grout, cream-colored
safety goggles
tile nipper
paintbrush
gloves
dry cloth

Instructions

1 | Affix the picture hangers securely to the back of the wooden board, and draw a sketch of your design onto the front.

2 | Plan the design and cut the tesserae according to the objects they will represent. For example, cut leaf-shaped tesserae for the leaves, and irregularly shaped tesserae for the bark. Use modeling clay to make the dates, and paint brown.

3 | When you are satisfied with the design, begin affixing the tesserae. Affix the branches, leaves, dates, and bark first, then affix the white, triangular shaped tesserae for the background. Affix square white tesserae all around the outer edge. Apply grout.

Design Tip

Look online for photos of a real date palm tree when sketching this design. Affix the dates first, then affix the tesserae that make up the branches and leaves.

Variations

The background in this image is monochromatic, but you can also create a landscape scene, using earthy colors for the bottom of the picture, and various shades of blue for the top.

Yuniah Goldwasser

Pomegranate Wall Hanging

36" x 20" (91 x 51 cm)

This tiny pomegranate is made up of a few red tesserae.

Use beads and gold glass to make one pomegranate that stands out from the rest.

Inspiration

This design features several ripe pomegranates, the thick-skinned red fruit that are cherished all over the world for their rich flavor and health properties. Pomegranates are known for their elegant crown and large number of seeds, and have been symbols of fertility since ancient times. In some traditions, it is believed that the number of seeds in a pomegranate is equal to the number of commandments in the Bible. Pomegranates are mentioned in many ancient texts, and described as beautiful fruit that are symbols of sweetness and goodness. In this mosaic rendition of the fruit, gold glass tesserae is used to create the crown on one of the fruit, and red beads are used to represent the seeds.

Materials & Tools

wooden board
steel picture hangers
sketching materials
ceramic tiles, various colors
glass, gold
beads
carpenter's wood glue
grout, white
safety goggles
tile nipper
glass cutter
paintbrush
gloves
dry cloth

Instructions

1 | Affix the picture hangers securely to the back of the wooden board, and draw a sketch of your design onto the front.

2 | Plan the design and cut the tesserae according to the objects they will represent. Note that the pomegranate in the bottom right corner features a crown made with gold glass tesserae, and a selection of red beads. The other pomegranates are made primarily from triangular ceramic tesserae.

3 | Affix the tesserae on the pomegranates and tree first, then affix the white and gray tesserae for the background. Affix square white tesserae all around the outer edge. Apply grout.

Design Tip

The tesserae in this design are cut to suit the elements they represent. Triangular tesserae are used to make the pomegranates, leaf-shaped tesserae are used to make the leaves, and rectangular tesserae are used for the bark.

Variations

Any fruit in season can be magnificent in mosaic. This technique can be used to make a close-up image of apples, oranges, or cherries ready for harvest. Base your design on a real tree, or use your imagination.

Moshit Segal

Memories of the Shore

24" (60 cm)

Combine handmade tiles shaped like sea creatures with real treasures from the sea.

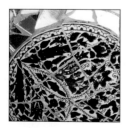

Round tiles with Armenian-style decals are surrounded with mirror tesserae.

Inspiration

Many people love collecting shells when they travel; this design is an excellent way of using them when you get home. The shells were collected from the shore near the artist's house, as well as faraway shores that the artist visited while traveling. To make sure the shells didn't long for their former marine home, the entire motif of this work relates to the sea. There are handmade ceramic tiles shaped like fish and starfish, and blue glass gems. The design also includes pieces of mirror, ceramic tiles with Armenian-style decals, and blue and white ceramic tiles. As for the jar itself, it features a wavy rim at the top, evocative of the waters of the sea.

Materials & Tools

ceramic jug
round ceramic tiles with Armenian-style decals
masking tape
ceramic tiles, various colors
handmade ceramic fish
shells
glass gems
ceramic glue
grout, blue
safety goggles
tile nipper
glass cutter
micro spatula
gloves
dry cloth

Instructions

1 | Plan your design and cut the tesserae. When cutting the round ceramic tiles with the Armenian-style decals, tape the tesserae together until you are ready to affix them, so that the designs are retained in the mosaic.

2 | When you are satisfied with the design, begin affixing the tesserae. Start with the round tiles located around the middle of the jug, then affix clusters of seashells at regular intervals around the jug. Surround these elements with randomly cut white and blue tesserae.

3 | At the top of the jug, affix rings of shells, ceramic fish, and glass gems. At the bottom of the jug, affix a ring of glass gems. Apply grout.

■ Design Tip

To create repeating patterns on this jug, arrange your shells in groups before affixing them to the pot, and make sure each group has shells in similar sizes.

■ Variations

If you have some particularly magnificent seashells you'd like to show off, affix them around the widest part of the jug, instead of the round ceramic tiles used in this design.

Moshit Segal

My Favorite Duck

18" x 12"
(45 x 30 cm)

Affix a ceramic rose on the top for a whimsical hat.

Inspiration

Garden shops sell a variety of giant cement animals which people often use to decorate their gardens and yards. Though these creatures are fine when left bare, they become fabulous when covered with mosaic designs. This giant duck features a wide range of tesserae that combine to create an eclectic playful impression. The beak is covered with bright red triangular tesserae, and the eyes are made from handmade ceramic roses. The feathers on the back are made from handmade ceramic leaves, and there are two necklaces made from bright glass gems. Ceramic figurines affixed on her back give her an even more eclectic look.

Materials & Tools

large ceramic duck
handmade ceramic roses
glass gems, various colors
glass, various colors
handmade ceramic leaves
ceramic figurines
ceramic tiles, various colors
grout, various colors
ceramic glue
safety goggles
tile cutters
glass cutter
gloves
dry cloth

Instructions

1 | Plan your design and cut the tesserae. Note that many of the tesserae in this design do not need to be cut, such as the ceramic leaves and the glass gems.

2 | When you are satisfied with the design, affix the tesserae. In this example, the tesserae are affixed in a relatively orderly manner. Handmade ceramic roses are affixed for the eyes, and these are encircled with white glass gems that cover the duck's face and upper neck. Below the white gems are several rings of gray glass gems, arranged in rings. Below this is a ring of rectangular yellow glass tesserae, then two more rings of glass gems.

3 | Affix handmade ceramic leaves so that they lie like feathers on the duck's back. Use triangular tesserae to decorate the duck's beak, belly, and tail, and use rectangular tesserae to decorate the feet. Affix glass gems for toenails, and ceramic figurines on the back. Apply grout.

■ Design Tip

Pay attention to detail when decorating this duck, as that's part of its charm. Use glass gems for the toenails and teeth, and ceramic roses to make the eyes and a hat.

■ Variations

This duck can take on a completely different look if you use different tesserae. Try using rings in different colors for a rainbow duck, or cover the entire duck in pebbles for a more natural look.

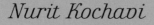

Nurit Kochavi

Window to My World

100" x 78" (2.54 x 1.98 m)

Surround each round ceramic tile with a border of rectangular mirror tesserae.

Inspiration

Looking for a way to update the exterior of your home without calling in the renovators? Try dressing up a wall with a colorful handmade mosaic. In this design, the mosaic was planned in sections, and assembled in my studio on nylon mesh. It was then transferred to the exterior wall of the artist's house. Using this technique, the artist was able to create a mosaic that was just perfect for her wall, and make all corrections to her design while working on the nylon mesh. The design features three bright suns below the window and a decorative area above the window. Several symbols for luck are also integrated into the design, providing her home with symbolic good fortune.

Materials & Tools

sketching materials
large piece of paper
acetate
nylon mesh
handmade flower tiles
handmade fish tiles
round ceramic tiles with Armenian-style decals
masking tape
ceramic tiles, various colored
decorative glass rounds
mirror
ceramic glue
hrout, gray
cement-based adhesive
measuring tape
scissors or sharp knife
tile nipper
glass cutter
micro spatula
gloves
dry cloth

Instructions

1 | Measure the dimensions of the window, and sketch your design on a large piece of paper. When you are satisfied with your sketch, lay it on your work surface, cover it with acetate, and lay the nylon mesh overtop.

2 | Cut the tesserae and plan your design. Arrange symmetrical elements at the same time, so that they are made in a similar manner. In this example, round tiles with Armenian-style decals are arranged in somewhat symmetrical columns on either side of the window, and surrounded by a random arrangement of colored tesserae. Three bright flowers are located below the window, and a wavy design is featured above it.

3 | When cutting the round Armenian-style ceramic tiles, tape the tiles together after they have been cut into until you are ready to affix.

4 | When you are satisfied with the design, affix the tesserae to the mesh. When the mosaic is dry, lift the mesh off the acetate, and affix on the wall. Apply grout.

Design Tip

Making a mosaic to affix on a wall surface requires careful planning. Double check the measurements of your design before you start affixing the tesserae, since you want it to be a perfect fit.

Variations

There are endless possibilities when decorating a wall. You can recreate a scene from a favorite story or song, imitate a beloved painting, or make a vertical field of flowers.

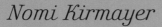

Nomi Kirmayer

Family of Feathered Friends

Duck: 16" x 8" (41 x 20 cm)
Chicken: 10" x 6" (25 x 15 cm)

Inspiration

This colorful collection of birds is made using simple clay figurines, similar to those sold in most garden centers. The roosters are decorated with several colors of bright glass tesserae: red tesserae are used for the crowns, green and red tesserae are used for the tail feathers, and an assortment of orange, green, and pink tesserae are used on the bodies. The duck features a slightly more elegant design than the roosters. Its body is covered with leaf-shaped white ceramic tesserae that are neatly arranged like feathers. The eyes are made from smooth glass gems, and the nose is made with heart-shaped tesserae. The duck's elegance is completed with its unusual crown of beads.

Materials & Tools

two rooster-shaped ceramic planters
duck-shaped planter
ceramic glue
ceramic rounds with eyes and hearts
glass, various colors
glass gems
ceramic tiles, various colors
grout, various colors
iron wire
glass beads
safety goggles
drill and drill bit
tile nipper
glass cutter
micro spatula
gloves
dry cloth

Instructions

1 | Drill small holes at the top of the duck for stringing the beaded wire. Plan your designs and cut the tesserae. Note that the duck in this example is decorated primarily with glass tesserae, and the roosters are decorated with ceramic tesserae.

2 | To decorate the roosters, affix the ceramic rounds with eyes and hearts first, then affix the tesserae all around. Use rounded tesserae for the roosters' crown and tail feathers. Apply grout.

3 | To decorate the duck, affix the glass gems in circles to form the eyes, then surround the eyes with triangular green tesserae. Decorate the rest of the body with leaf-shaped white tesserae. Apply grout.

4 | To make the duck's crown of beads, draw wire through the holes at the top of the duck's head, then string on an assortment of beads. Twist the wires into loops at the top of the head to secure. Apply grout.

■ Design Tip

Prepare tesserae for both roosters at the same time, so that you can make them similar but different. When decorating the duck, select tesserae for the face that complement those used in the crown of beads.

■ Variations

Ceramic planters come in a variety of animals shapes. Choose any creatures that suit your garden, and select tesserae that match.

Feminine Figure with Roses

28" x 16" (70 x 40 cm)

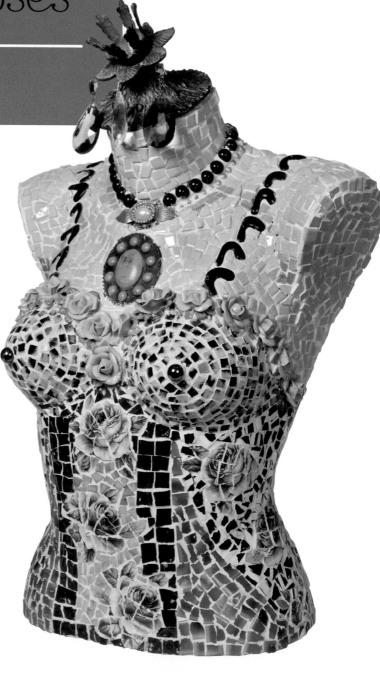

Carefully arranged marbles
make an elegant choker.

The marble necklace
continues around the back of
the figure too.

Inspiration

When shaping the clay to make this figure, I felt as though I was making an extraordinary woman, and wanted to create a mosaic outfit that was suitably beautiful and striking. This mosaic features an old belt buckle and brooch, the base of a light fixture, and a couple of earrings made from chandelier crystals. It also features an assortment of roses that I salvaged from old napkin holders, and roses that were cut from tiles with decals. In addition to using materials found at a flea market, I also incorporated items that I bought at a dollar store, including the marbles that were used to make the necklace, and the U-shaped glass pieces that make up the shirt straps.

Materials & Tools

handmade ceramic female bust
marbles
pearls
turquoise belt buckle
silver and pearl brooch
porcelain flowers
U-shaped pieces of glass
ceramic tiles with rose decals
masking tape
ceramic tiles, various colors
ceramic glue
grout, white
metal light fixture
chandelier crystals
safety goggles
tile nipper
micro spatula
gloves
dry cloth

Instructions

1 | Plan your design and prepare the tesserae. In this example, several tesserae do not need to be cut at all. These tesserae include the marbles and pearls used to make the necklace and the U-shaped pieces of glass used to make the straps.

2 | To prepare tesserae from the ceramic tiles with the rose decals, cut out the roses and leaves so that they look like they are cut from paper, then cut the roses into randomly shaped tesserae. Tape the tesserae together until you are ready to affix, so that the roses are retained in the mosaic.

3 | When you are satisfied with the design, affix the tesserae. Affix symmetrical elements at the same time, so that they are made in a similar manner. Apply grout. Affix the metal light fixture at the neck of the figure and hang the chandelier crystals.

■ Design Tip

Affix the larger tesserae first, then use the smaller tesserae to fill in the spaces. Highlight a few extraordinary tesserae by affixing them in the middle, as a necklace or brooch.

■ Variations

This figure features eclectic tesserae including ceramic roses, children's marbles, and chandelier crystals. If you'd prefer a more staid look, use tesserae from ceramic tiles to make your outfit.

My Hobby Horse

Ayelet Shemesh

20" x16" x 6"
(50 x 40 x 15 cm)

Combine handmade flowers with large pearly beads for a beautiful and striking saddle.

Inspiration

Many people dream of having a horse. With this design, you can have a horse of your very own, without having to find a stable or procure fresh hay. This beautiful mare is made from a rusty metal horse that was purchased for a steal in a flea market. The original horse likely spent several years outdoors subject to the elements, but receives much better treatment in its renewed form. The horse is covered with a saddle of handmade ceramic flowers and leaves, and large pearly beads. The glass that was used to make up its coat is a rich burgundy color. As for the face and tail, these are decorated with ceramic tiles in various shapes and sizes.

Materials & Tools

large metal horse
handmade ceramic flowers
handmade ceramic leaves
ceramic tiles, various shapes
large pearly beads
glass, burgundy
silicone acrylic glue with dispenser
safety goggles
glass cutters
micro spatula

Instructions

1 | Plan your design and cut the tesserae. In this example, the horse's saddle features an assortment of handmade flowers and leaves, and large pearly beads. The tail features pearly beads and a few ceramic tesserae, and the face features a couple ceramic tiles in various shapes. As for the rest of the figure, it is covered in square-shaped glass tesserae.

2 | When you are satisfied with the design, affix the tesserae.

Design Tip

Arrange the tesserae on the saddle, tail, and face first, then decorate the rest of the body. Be sure to cover the legs all around, and the underside of the horse's belly.

Variations

This horse is covered in glass tesserae, but you can also decorate it with colorful ceramic tiles, with or without decals.

Gali Kamile

Candelabrum with Pomegranates

17" x 13" x 13"
(42 x 32 x 32 cm)

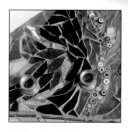

Arrange the millefiori beads so that they flow from the pomegranates to the candle cups.

Inspiration

This nine-branched candelabrum is cut from two wooden boards that are affixed together at a perpendicular angle. It features a pair of pomegranates that symbolize fertility, richness, and good health. These are decorated in vibrant colors of glass that emphasize this association. Eight small candle cups are affixed at equal intervals along two sides of the triangular base, and a ninth candle cup is positioned atop a small glass triangle at the tip of the base. The mosaic design, comprised of glass tesserae and millefiori beads, extends from the pomegranates on the back to the triangular base. A trim of square blue tesserae is affixed all around the base of the candelabrum.

Materials & Tools

wooden board
sketching materials
nails
nine small candle cups
carpenter's wood glue
small glass triangle
glass, various colors
millefiori glass beads
gray grout
hammer
paintbrush
safety goggles
glass cutter
gloves
dry cloth

Instructions

1 | Draw a triangle and two pomegranates on the wooden boards and have a carpenter cut the boards. Secure the pomegranate-shaped piece to the longest edge of the triangle, so that it is perpendicular to the triangular base.

2 | Position eight of the candle cups so that they are evenly spaced along the two shorter edges of the triangle, and affix. Affix the glass triangle at the tip of the base, and affix the remaining candle cup on top.

3 | Plan your design and cut the tesserae. Note that the colors of the tesserae used in the pomegranates flow in a continuous stream onto the base. Plan for an area on the triangle for affixing the millefiori beads.

4 | When you are satisfied with the design, affix the tesserae. Affix small blue square tesserae around the edge. Apply grout.

Design Tip

When decorating the pomegranates, lay the candelabrum on its back, so that the pomegranates are flat on your work surface. After this area is dry, position the candelabrum upright, and decorate the base.

Variations

Select any image you like for the background of this work. Trees, animals, and fruit are all excellent subjects for such a piece.

Earthenware Candleholder

16" (40 cm)

The rim of each hole is
decorated with carefully
cut tesserae.

Inspiration

This decorative candle holder was made from an ordinary ceramic pot that, due to a couple of deep cracks, was for sale at a much reduced price at a garden center. I took advantage of the cracks to drill three circular holes near the top of the pot, and made elegant borders of peach-colored glass tesserae around each hole. The rim at the top of the pot is decorated with wave-shaped tesserae. As for the mosaic design on the rest of the pot, it is made from tesserae that are cut in a seemingly random manner. The flowers and leaves on the base of the pot were salvaged from kitchen wall tiles in a house that was scheduled for renovations.

Materials & Tools

- ceramic plant pot
- glass, peach
- ceramic tiles with floral decals
- masking tape
- ceramic glue
- grout, beige
- safety goggles
- drill and masonry drill bit
- glass cutter
- tile nipper
- micro spatula
- gloves
- dry cloth

Instructions

1 | Drill three large holes around the top of the pot to make three round windows.

2 | Plan your design and cut the tesserae. Cut the peach-colored glass into square tesserae for affixing around the windows. As for the ceramic tiles with floral decals, these are cut in a random manner, but areas featuring flowers are taped together after they are cut, and until they are affixed onto the pot, so that the flowers can be reassembled on the pot.

3 | When you are satisfied with the design, affix the tesserae. Apply grout.

Design Tip

Affix the floral elements first, then fill in the spaces with background tesserae. When choosing the tesserae to surround the windows, select a color that complements the floral decals.

Variations

You can use this simple technique to enhance pots of any shape and size. You can also make as many holes as you like. Several pots decorated in this manner make excellent garden lamps.

Mediterranean Cityscape

24" x 28" (60 x 70 cm)

Inspiration

This landscape design is inspired by a view of Jerusalem, one of the most remarkable cities in the world. Each element is made from different colored tesserae cut in different manners. Triangular tesserae are used to depict the roofs, and a variety of blue tesserae, arranged in a seemingly random manner, are used for the sky. The design also includes a number of handmade elements, such the ceramic decorations used to decorate the doors in the yellow building, the red tulip nestled between the two yellow buildings, and a couple of blue stars. I chose a golden frame for this work, to enhance the sense of richness and opulence.

Materials & Tools

wooden board

sketching materials

ceramic tiles, various colors

handmade imprinted ceramic tiles

glass, various colors

handmade ceramic shapes

carpenter's wood glue

gold matting and frame

safety goggles

tile nipper

glass cutter

paintbrush

Instructions

1 | Draw a sketch of your design onto the board.

2 | Plan the design and cut the tesserae according to the objects they will represent. For example, cut triangular tesserae for roofs, and square tesserae for building bricks.

3 | When you are satisfied with the design, affix the tesserae. Have a professional framer frame the mosaic.

Design Tip

Select different colors of tile for each building, and cut the tiles into tesserae of distinct shapes.

Variations

This technique can be used to transfer any landscape into the mosaic medium. Look at a postcard or photograph for inspiration, then sketch the main elements of the scene onto the wooden board.

Gali Kamile

Mask with Red Hair

41" x 20" (105 x 50 cm)

The inspiration for this work is a handmade ceramic mask.

Inspiration

The main image in this work is the ceramic mask in its center, an object that was designed by the artist in my studio. The mask features a face, looking forward, that is divided into four parts. While the mask is in natural, earthy hues, the tesserae used to make the hair and cover the wooden background are bright and colorful, providing a striking contrast to the colors of the mask. The tesserae in the background include rich reds, bright oranges, and regal golds. The hair above the mask was shaped using modeling clay, and is covered with various shades of red tesserae. Both the hair and the mask protrude from the surface of the work, adding another dimension.

Materials & Tools

- wooden board
- steel picture hangers
- handmade ceramic mask
- carpenter's wood glue
- sketching materials
- modeling clay
- ceramic tiles, various colors
- glass, various tiles
- ceramic glue
- paintbrush
- safety goggles
- glass cutter
- tile nippers
- micro spatula

Instructions

1 | Affix the picture hangers securely to the back of the wooden board. Affix the mask to the front of the board, and draw a sketch of your design around the mask.

2 | Build up the three wavy areas above the mask with modeling clay. These areas will be covered with red tesserae, for the hair.

3 | Plan your design and cut the tesserae. When you are satisfied with the design, affix the tesserae. Be sure to use appropriate glues for the different surfaces. Start by affixing the tesserae onto the modeling clay relief, then work your way outward, until the entire board is covered.

■ Design Tip

Affix tesserae onto the areas built up with modeling clay first. Be sure to decorate the edges of these areas, also, so that the modeling clay is completely covered.

■ Variations

If you don't have a handmade ceramic mask for this project, try using a wooden mask. You can also build a mask directly onto the wooden board using modeling clay. Brush it with white glue for a shiny finish.

Gali Kamile

Pomegranate Trio

8" x 10" (20 x 25 cm) each

Inspiration

These three bright fruits were designed to match Candelabrum with Pomegranates on page 92. They were cut from small pieces of wood that were left over from other projects. (Nothing goes to waste in my studio). Each pomegranate is decorated with various colors of glass tesserae, but although each pomegranate has its own color scheme, all three are linked in shape and design. Each pomegranate features a cluster of three leaf-shaped tesserae at its bottom, a shape that links up with the three-pronged crown at the top. All of the tesserae along the edges of the pomegranates are carefully cut to preserve the shape of each pomegranate.

Materials & Tools

wooden boards
steel picture hangers
sketching materials
glass, various colors
carpenter's wood glue
grout, gray
steel picture hangers
safety goggles
glass cutter
paintbrush
gloves
dry cloth

Instructions

1 | Draw three pomegranates onto the wooden boards and have a carpenter cut the boards. Affix picture hangers to the back of each pomegranate.

2 | Plan your designs and cut the tesserae. Note that the tesserae around the edge of each pomegranate are cut carefully to maintain the shape of the pomegranate.

3 | When you are satisfied with the designs, affix the tesserae. Apply grout.

■ Design Tip

Take care when cutting the glass tesserae for the edges of these fruit, and try to make the curves as smooth as possible.

■ Variations

This idea can be translated to any selection of fruit. Pears, apples, and cherries all have distinct shapes that can be recreated in multiple small mosaics for a lovely and unique wall design.

Meirav Kleinberg

Date Palm Tree Frame

39" x 28" (100 x 70 cm)

Inspiration

This frame recreates the beauty and lushness of palm trees rich with ripe dates. It features an immense variety of tesserae, all of which were selected for their ability to convey a certain impression. For example, the tesserae in the tree bark are cut in diverse rounded shapes to resemble the texture of a real palm tree; the leaves are made from leaf-shaped tesserae, and arranged in a symmetrical manner similar to how they occur in nature; real pebbles are affixed along the base of the design. Two types of dates appear in this design: there are clusters of ceramic dates affixed near the bark of each tree and hanging dates made from gold wire strung with brown beads.

Materials & Tools

- wooden board
- steel picture hangers
- sketching materials
- ceramic tiles, various colors
- handmade imprinted ceramic tiles
- handmade ceramic dates
- pebbles
- grout, various colors
- brown beads
- gold metal wire
- safety goggles
- tile nipper
- glass cutter
- paintbrush
- wire cutters
- gloves
- dry cloth

Instructions

1 | Draw an outline of the desired frame onto the wooden board, and have a carpenter cut the board. Affix the picture hangers securely to the back of the board, and drill a few holes on branches in both trees for hanging dates.

2 | Plan your design and cut the tesserae. Cut leaf-shaped green tesserae for the leaves, rounded tesserae from various brown ceramic tiles for the bark, and randomly shaped tesserae from handmade ceramic tiles imprinted with lace for the sky. You'll use a combination of real pebbles and ceramic tesserae for decorating the bottom of the design. Set aside areas for affixing the ceramic dates.

3 | When you are satisfied with the design, affix the tesserae. Affix the ceramic dates in clusters. Apply grout. String brown beads onto several pieces of gold metal wire and string the wires through the holes that were drilled in the branches. Have a professional framer mount the frame securely onto the mirror.

Design Tip

Start collecting pebbles for the bottom of this design well in advance, because you'll want them in a variety of shapes and sizes.

Variations

You can make this mirror with any pair of trees you like, just consider alternative materials for depicting the fruit. For example, if you make apple or cherry trees, try dangling round red glass beads for the fruit.

Meirav Kleinberg

Garden Bench with Poinsettias

59" x 22" (150 x 55 cm)

Pieces of red and black glass are cut with precision to make this flower.

Inspiration

This bench is based upon an old wrought iron bench that someone was giving away for free after it failed to sell at a garage sale. The back of the bench was preserved, but a new seat and arms were soldered on. Decorated with a vibrant floral motif, this bench ensures that there are flowers in the artist's garden all year long. The seat of the bench features two vibrant poinsettias. A single rectangular board on the back of the bench features a flower that is similar to the flowers on the seat. The armrests are decorated with swirling lines of tesserae and glass gems. Note that the petals and leaves of the large poinsettias were cut precisely using pistol grip cutters commonly used in stained glass.

Materials & Tools

- wrought-iron bench, custom-designed to support wooden boards
- wooden boards, cut to fit wrought-iron bench
- sketching materials
- glass, various colors
- glass gems
- carpenter's wood glue
- grout, gray
- screws
- safety goggles
- glass cutter
- pistol grip cutters
- paintbrush
- gloves
- dry cloth
- screwdriver

Instructions

1 | Draw sketches of your designs onto the boards.

2 | Plan the design and cut the tesserae. Note that the petals and leaves on the largest boards are cut with precision using pistol grip cutters.

3 | When you are satisfied with the designs, affix the tesserae onto the boards. When making the boards that will be used for the seat, affix the petals and leaves first, then fill in the spaces with randomly cut tesserae. When making the armrests, affix the blue tesserae and glass gems first, then affix white tesserae for the background. Apply grout.

4 | Fit the wooden boards into the appropriate areas on the bench and secure with screws.

▣ Design Tip

Practice using the pistol grip cutters before cutting out the flower petals in this design. When decorating the largest wooden boards, affix the flower petals and leaves first, then affix the background tesserae.

▣ Variations

This bench would look lovely with golden sunflowers or bright gerberas as well. Simply select the flower of your choice, and choose high quality glass that will do justice to your design.

Michal Ma'oz

Sunshine Bench with Figure

217" x 20" x 20"
(550 x 50 x 50 cm)

Inspiration

Anyone who has been to Barcelona, or seen pictures of its most famous sites, will likely recognize the influence of Antoni Gaudí in this design. It is a wavy concrete bench decorated with boldly colored tesserae that are arranged in the shapes of lizards, flowers, and a bright sunshine. This mosaic was constructed on nylon mesh in my studio, then transferred to a concrete bench that had been made especially for this project. The mosaic man sitting at one end of the bench was also made for this project. Usually, he sits at leisure in his tidy suit of ceramic tesserae and contemplates the world. He can also be removed from the bench at will, to make room for real people.

Materials & Tools

handmade concrete bench

sketching materials

large pieces of paper

acetate

nylon mesh

ceramic tiles, various colors

ceramic tiles with floral decals

ceramic adhesive

grout

handmade ceramic figure with a top hat

measuring tape

scissors or sharp knife

safety goggles

tile nipper

glass cutter

micro spatula

gloves

dry cloth

Instructions

1 | Measure the dimensions of the concrete bench, and sketch your design on paper. Since this design is three dimensional, you will want to use separate sheets of paper for each dimension, while ensuring that the design on every sheet is connected. When you are satisfied with your sketch, lay it on your work surface, cover it with acetate, and lay nylon mesh overtop

2 | Cut the tesserae and plan your design. In this example, red, orange, and yellow tesserae tiles are used to create the sunshine. Tesserae in various shades of brown are used to make the lizards, and green tesserae are used to make leaves. There are also several flowers on the bench made from ceramic tiles with floral decals.

3 | When you are satisfied with the design, affix the tesserae to the mesh. When the mosaic is dry, lift the mesh off the acetate, and affix onto the bench. Apply grout.

4 | To make the figure in the top hat, use green tesserae for the pants, black and yellow tesserae for the jacket, and red tesserae for the hat. Plan your design, then affix the tesserae. Apply grout.

■ Design Tip

Carefully measure the sheets you use as the base for this design, since you want everything to line up properly when the mosaic is affixed to the bench.

■ Variations

Since the style of this garden bench is inspired by Antoni Gaudí, take a look of some of his other works for inspiration. If you like, replace the figure sitting on the bench with a mosaic cat, bird, or lizard.

Tzofi Peled

Dresser of Victorian Dreams

39" x 24" (100 x 60 cm)

Surrounding these angels with pearls enhances their heavenly appearance.

Inspiration

Although most furniture is made to be functional, there is no law that says functional furniture can't be beautiful, too. The dresser used in this work functioned perfectly, but left something to be desired when it came to beauty. A variety of Victorian elements were incorporated into the design, including cherubic angels, roses that were cut carefully from ceramic tiles, and a treasure trove of pearls. The dresser also includes a selection of handmade ceramic roses that add relief to the work. Green tesserae are used to decorate the front of every drawer and are surrounded with a border of rectangular black tesserae. Large green tesserae are affixed on the top of the dresser.

Materials & Tools

wooden three-drawer dresser
sketching materials
ceramic tiles with angel decals
round ceramic tiles with floral decals
pearls, various sizes
handmade ceramic roses
ceramic tiles, various colors
glass, green
carpenter's wood glue
grout, green
sandpaper
safety goggles
tile nipper
glass cutter
paintbrush
gloves
dry cloth

Instructions

1 | Sand down the dresser until it is smooth. Draw a sketch of your design onto the dresser, concentrating on the placement of the angels, roses, and pearls.

2 | When you are satisfied with the design, cut the tesserae. Cut the ceramic tiles with angel and rose decals so that these elements look like they are cut from paper. Cut rectangular-shaped black ceramic tesserae for affixing in borders around each drawer. Cut green ceramic tesserae to decorate the front of the drawers, and larger glass tesserae to decorate the top.

3 | Affix the rectangular black tesserae around each of the drawers. Affix one angel on each drawer, then affix the pearls so that they surround the angels and form a continuous stream of pearls running from the top drawer, through the middle drawer, and onto the bottom drawer. Affix the handmade ceramic roses and flowers that were cut from ceramic tiles. Finally affix ceramic green tesserae to make the background on the drawers, and green glass tesserae in the top of the dresser. Apply grout on the drawers.

■ **Design Tip**

Arrange the beads that surround the angels so that they create a continuous flow between the three drawers. If you think you'll be placing lots of things on the top of the dresser, you may want to leave this area bare.

■ **Variations**

Change the theme of this dresser to suit any room décor. Decorate it with tiles that have animals, bright flowers, birds, or butterflies for a children's room.

Eve in the Garden

67" x 20" (170 x 50 cm)

Colorful ceramic birds add a whimsical touch to this thought-provoking piece.

The snake winds around the back of the figure as well.

Inspiration

The theme of this work is Eve in the Garden of Eden, as evident in the presence of an apple tree, a snake, and an unclad female figure. The mosaic on the figure features blue tesserae to imitate the skies that were visible in Eden, as well as heart-shaped red fruit that evoke the forbidden fruit of the Tree of Knowledge. Note that the figure's chest is made from a plastic apple that is cut in half, linking the materials used to make this work with its theme. A group of playful birds is affixed at the top of the figure, and a mischievous-looking elf is positioned at the base.

Materials & Tools

large ceramic pot
partial mannequin
ceramic glue
plastic apple, cut in half
polyurethane foam
ceramic tiles with snakeskin decals
ceramic tiles, various colors
small ceramic birds
small ceramic elf
micro spatula
safety goggles
tile nipper
gloves
dry cloth

Instructions

1 | Position the ceramic pot so that it forms a stable base, and affix the mannequin securely on top.

2 | Affix the plastic apple halves at chest level. To make the base for the snake, spray polyurethane in thick winding strip around the figure.

3 | Plan your design and cut the tesserae. In this example, tesserae made from ceramic tiles with snakeskin decals are used to cover the snake. Leaf-shaped green tesserae are used for the leaves, and heart-shaped red tesserae are used for the apples. The base of the figure features diverse brown tesserae, and the top features various shades of blue tesserae.

4 | When you are satisfied with the design, affix the tesserae. Apply grout. Affix the ceramic birds at the top of the figure, and the elf figure at the bottom.

Design Tip

Affix tesserae to the snake's body first, then affix to the rest of the figure. Make sure the tesserae along the edge of the snake's body have a precise edge, distinguishing the snake from the figure.

Variations

If you don't have a mannequin to use for constructing this body, consider building it on inverted vases, such as those that were used to make the sisters on pages 52 and 54.